THE
Big PICTURE

THE
Big PICTURE

Filmmaking Lessons
from a Life on the Set

TOM REILLY

THOMAS DUNNE BOOKS
ST. MARTIN'S PRESS ❦ NEW YORK

THOMAS DUNNE BOOKS.
An Imprint of St. Martin's Press.

THE BIG PICTURE. Copyright © 2009 by Tom Reilly. All rights reserved. Printed
in the United States of America. For information, address St. Martin's
Press, 175 Fifth Avenue, New York, N.Y. 10010.

www.thomasdunnebooks.com
www.stmartins.com

Design by Elina D. Nudelman

Library of Congress Cataloging-in-Publication Data

Reilly Tom A.
    The big picture : filmmaking lessons from a life on the set / Tom Reilly.—
1st ed.
        p.   cm.
    "Thomas Dunne Books."
    Includes bibliographical references and index.
    ISBN-13: 978-0-312-38038-0
    ISBN-10: 0-312-38038-0
    1. Motion pictures—Production and direction. 2. Cinematography. I.
Title.
    PN1995.9.P7R378 2009
    791.4302'32—dc22
                                                                2008044615

First Edition: May 2009

10 9 8 7 6 5 4 3 2 1

For James, Kate, and Mackenzie

CONTENTS

CONTENTS

CONTENTS

CONTENTS

ACKNOWLEDGMENTS

FIRST and foremost, I'd like to acknowledge the hundreds of filmmakers whose names appear in the credits of the films I've worked on and who took the time to share their knowledge with me during the course of my career. Their friendship means a lot to me.

I would like to thank Peter Joseph, my editor at Thomas Dunne Books, for his enthusiasm and insight, and for making the writing process so enjoyable for me.

Thanks also to my agent, Helena Schwarz, for her perseverance and guidance; to Brian Hamill for his friendship and great photography; to Phil Caruso for his kind and valuable advice; and to Melissa Tomjanovich for her help and efficiency.

Finally, I'd like to thank my wife, Kathy, and my children, James, Kate, and Mackenzie, for their inspiration and support.

I still believe that the best possible school is the film set.

—BERNARDO BERTOLUCCI

THE Big PICTURE

PREFACE

MAKING a feature film is a lot like raising a teenager. It's not only exhausting, it's almost impossible to do well. At one time or another, both endeavors become, at least briefly, unrecognizable even to those of us present at their conception. Both tasks are prohibitively expensive, take on a life of their own, and evoke more criticism than praise. While they begin as cherished and beloved projects, and are nurtured and embraced with great expectation, the process of filmmaking, like that of parenting, is always daunting. Somewhere along the way, both film and child go through a transitional and sometimes difficult stage. Then, through diligence, perseverance, and a bit of blind faith, they hopefully become, once again, worthy of our devotion and evolve into something to be proud of. Or at the very least, upon reflection, the experience is one we can think back on without cringing.

Which brings me to one of the most important things I know about filmmaking: *If it's not in the shot, it doesn't matter. . . .* While the process of filmmaking, like that of parenting, leaves us drowning in the pedestrian, in the tedium of day-to-day details, to succeed, we must remember the big picture. It is easy to lose sight of the finished project when we can't see past the twelve-hour day it may take to shoot just part of a single scene, or the two extra days we need and don't have to do the work, or that location we just lost. *If it's not in the shot, it*

1

doesn't matter. I've said it to Barbra Streisand, Irwin Winkler, and many a first-time director.

I realize that this, like so many of the other tenets of good filmmaking, I learned on the set with Woody Allen. These indelible truths were gleaned from the master himself, over almost two decades, then etched in stone by the great cinematographers Gordon Willis, Carlo Di Palma, and Sven Nykvist. The spoken and unspoken axioms were learned and relearned over the course of eighteen films, from *Stardust Memories* to *Mighty Aphrodite.* They provide insight for both film viewer and filmmaker alike, and hold true whether you're sitting in a theater, making your first student film, or shooting a career-capping, big-budget studio picture.

So here they are, my self-proclaimed commandments of great filmmaking, covering both the creative and technical, the groundbreaking and the mundane. *Shoot in flat light. Keep the script to one hundred pages. Sweat the small stuff. Pick your ten best shots. Shoot on a low floor. Move the camera. Assume nothing. Recognize the power of a single line. Have a nice lunch.* And of course, because art imitates life: *If it's not in the shot, it doesn't matter.*

1

LEARN THE VOCABULARY OF FILM.

IT'S three o'clock in the morning. I'm standing on the boardwalk in Asbury Park, a community on the New Jersey shore that has seen better days. It is twelve degrees out, and though I am clad in Gore-Tex and goose down and fleece, the January wind off the ocean is cutting right through my clothes and skin.

I am surrounded by a seventy-five-member film crew, tons of equipment, and have only four hours and eighteen minutes until the sun comes up. Despite the cold, I am holding a walkie-talkie in my bare hand because I can't press the "talk" button down or turn the knobs with my gloves on. When I make the call, "First team's ready," a thought flashes through my mind. It is not "Will the camera freeze?" or "Will the dialogue be audible above the wind?" It is not "Will Robert De Niro and James Franco be able to navigate the icy boardwalk and deliver a performance in these conditions?" It is far more self-indulgent. At this moment, steeped in exhaustion and biting cold, I ask myself, How did I end up here? And I realize it is because I didn't want to wear a necktie.

When I got out of college and my peers headed off to Brooks Brothers and Wall Street, I knew only that one thing: that I didn't want to wear a tie to work. So I started reading *Variety* and noticed a small ad in the back announcing a training program offered by the Directors Guild of America. A few phone calls and a written application landed me in New York City, where I took a series of entrance exams given by the Directors Guild for a spot in a two-year training program for assistant directors. I had only a vague sense of what an assistant director did, but it sounded promising.

Of the nearly one thousand applicants, only seven of us were selected, and I was assigned to the first film to start up in New York that autumn. When I walked into the production office on day one in my white shirt and creased pants, I still wasn't wearing a tie, but I did feel something tightening around my neck. Not silk perhaps, but apprehension. I knew I had a lot to learn.

Film students and filmmakers often talk about the language of film—the lenses, method of framing, and shot selection—that are the brick and mortar of our trade. But I didn't learn this vocabulary and grammar from textbooks with pages of diagrams depicting camera angles, or by discussing blocking, aspect ratios, and the benefits and limitations of standard coverage while sitting in a classroom. I wasn't inundated with essays enumerating the mechanics of screen direction or the philosophy behind New Wave cinema and Jean-Luc Godard's use of close-ups, or Hitchcock's high angles, Kurosawa's preference for long lenses, or Fellini's brilliance. Instead, I learned what is referred to as the vocabulary of film in the total immersion of a film set.

I learned about long lenses and depth of field not from the course material handed out second semester, or during a day spent at the library with film journals, but from the syllabus of a long string of ten-week shoots on the streets of New York. My education occurring not over a few semesters, but over a few decades. Taught to me, not by professors in a classroom, but by filmmakers with dolly track at their feet and their eye to a viewfinder. My understanding of the differences between the styles of European and American filmmakers, explained not in the theoretical secondhand words of a textbook, but by the thick, accented voices I can still hear in my head; Lajos Koltai, Miroslav Ondrícek, Juan Ruiz Anchía. . . . The Europeans' love for the zoom lens; its simplicity, its versatility and freedom, the fluidity of a single shot demonstrated as I witnessed its use in the hands of Giuseppe Rotunno and Sven Nykvist. Then there's Woody's masterful blocking, Emmanuel Lubezki's inspired lighting (*Great Expectations*), Carlo Di Palma's camera movement (*Hannah and Her Sisters*), and Gordon Willis's framing and technique (*Stardust Memories*).

I discovered the converging and dichotomous styles of the American and British cinematographers firsthand. The years and pictures come streaming back in the voices of Billy Williams (*Going in Style*) and Gerry Fisher (*Lovesick*). One could argue that the British style of working, where the director of photography (DP) has less involvement in actual shot design than an American cinematographer would, and is more of a lighting director, leaving the operator to work with the director designing shots, may not be the best system. But a quick look at the bodies of work of the great British DPs and the argument fades. Think about Billy Williams and *Gandhi*, or *On Golden Pond* and *Eleni*.

Which brings me back to Asbury Park and that boardwalk in New Jersey. The movie is *City by the Sea* and I am the assistant director (AD). Which doesn't mean I'm the guy fetching lattes for the director. It means I am the filmmaking professional running the set and managing the day-to-day operations of the movie. My job begins several months prior to shooting, in preproduction, when the movie is nothing more than a director, a script, and possibly a leading actor. As the cast and crew are hired, I break down the script, dissecting every scene into its component parts—location, actors, props. Then I schedule the film, scout locations, and, in coordination with a team of production people, create a plan to bring the project from conceptual idea to physical execution, from movie script to movie screen. On day one of shooting, I become a field general of sorts as we take over entire city blocks with a virtual army of talent and trucks and equipment.

Early in my career, Wolfgang Glattes, another assistant director, took a moment to explain about the compression that occurs with a long lens, creating the illusion that two objects are closer together than they really are. Two boats on a river, two cars on a street, can be made to appear to almost collide without ever coming very close to each other. In that instant, with that tiny piece of film vocabulary, a mere fraction of what I would need to know about the 150-mm lens, I learned that drama, which is so often the result of an actor's performance and delivery of lines, can also be created by a camera lens. Think of the impact, the independent and combined effect that blocking, number of frames shot per second, field size, camera height, and editing techniques can have on the drama, the suspense, the comedic timing of your story. What lens do you want on the camera? What filters? How is the camera mounted? What happens if you dolly in and zoom in simultaneously, or dolly in and zoom out? If you don't know, you will find your choices limited. I recall Alfonso Cuarón's *(A Little Princess, Y Tu Mamá También)* simple observation that if you're filming on an ugly set, go to a long lens. Only the actors will be in sharp focus and everything else will be soft.

I learned screen direction, knowing who should be looking camera right or camera left and why, while standing just a few feet from a camera, next to some of the greatest cinematographers in the world. The absolute necessity of matching an actor's visual direction is as significant as the choreography of a fight scene, where glances, rather than punches, are laid out with precision. Think of the complicated screen direction mandated by a sequence with multiple actors sitting around a table conversing. Then consider the brilliant shot in *Manhattan Murder Mystery* as the camera circles five actors around a table at Elaine's, all covered in a single 270-degree shot. The scene photographed in a way that gave complete freedom from the necessity to match for screen direction. The next time you are watching a film or television commercial, notice how often directors get the eye lines wrong. The sloppy work evidenced by actors looking the wrong way when the footage is cut together.

From both the explicit and the tacit knowledge gleaned from hundreds of professional filmmakers, I acquired a fluency and competence in the language of film. I can diagram a scene like a writer can diagram a sentence, because I know both the proper grammar and the street slang of film. I know the lenses, their depth of field, and when or when not to use them.

Whether you learn the vocabulary of film sitting in a classroom or standing on a set, your goal should be technical fluency. Once this is acquired, you then have the freedom to break the rules of perfect grammar, as Jean-Luc Godard did in 1960 in *Breathless* when he cut out small pieces of film, removing frames at odd moments, leaving the timing visibly off and a little jarring. The editing of *Breathless* is analogous to a visual arrhythmia, a sentence fragment for the screen, or a syncopated jazz line, a little ragtime for the eye. Or consider something as mundane as mounting a camera on a couple of two-by-fours and creating what Barry Sonnenfeld called the "whacky-cam" on *Big,* when he wanted to create a shot that amounted to a paddleball's "point of view" as it flew toward a cement wall. Two grips ran with the camera mounted on the two-by-fours, fitted with an extremely wide-angle lens to eliminate any jiggling—as the camera traced the ball's path.

The Big Picture

Then examine the handheld camerawork designed by Woody and Carlo Di Palma for *Husbands and Wives* and look at Thomas Vinterberg's *The Celebration,* the revolutionary work produced when a group of Danish filmmakers (Dogme 95) decided to break all the rules and change the vocabulary of film. Or perhaps you will become fluent enough to be able to recognize a roughly translated piece of the vocabulary of film outside of a movie screen, as director Arne Glimcher (*The Mambo Kings, Just Cause*) theorized he did when he noticed a parallel between elements of early cinema and the development of Cubism. He saw a striking similarity between the signature jumpy and fragmented movement of the cinematograph used in the early days of the Paris movie houses and what had emerged on the sketchpads and the canvases of Braque and Picasso. This led him to speculate that the jagged and jarring images of early film might possibly have been a contributing factor in the development of this revolutionary new style of art and the "fractured" movement seen in the work of these early Cubist painters. An impossible observation to make without a fluency in the vocabulary of film.

Each of these respected artists is contributing something of their own, something unsettling, unexpected, unconventional, controversial, to the vocabulary and the art of filmmaking.

The job of a filmmaker is to take a story and translate it into the language of cinema. Without a fluency in the vocabulary and grammar of filmmaking, it is an overwhelming task. So if you want to be a filmmaker, learn the language of film, the lenses, screen direction and blocking, shot composition and editing techniques. Learn it in the classroom or on the set, or begin to learn it here in the pages of this book, but learn it so well that eventually you can break some of the rules, leave the punctuation off, and follow the path of the great filmmakers and write something new.

2

LEARN THE LANGUAGE OF THE SET.

THE first time you step onto a movie set may leave you feeling like you have just landed in a foreign country. Not only because of the unfamiliar terrain of the set, the strange landscape of equipment and personnel, of cables and trucks and costumes, but because of the distinct language spoken there. Although initially recognizable, it is oddly incomprehensible, despite the litany of familiar words. What emerges is an unusual dialect, peppered with the hybrid language of film. A redhead, a blonde. Not what you think. A trombone, a banjo. Clearly not musical instruments. A doughnut, a pancake, a quarter apple. Obviously not references to food. A bazooka, a finger, a pigeon, a fish pole, barn doors, a giraffe, an elephant ear. Not a single one of these words decipherable in the context of how it is being used.

As you try to navigate around these terms, you then stumble upon a whole new set of completely unfamiliar words and odd utterances. The technical speak, the idiosyncrasies and jargon of our motion-picture patois.

The words: an inky-dink, a basher, a Winnie, a wigwag, a scrim. Italian track, flocking paper, a gyro. Duvetyn, a cookaloris. The phrases and questions: Check the gate. Do you want the split diopter? Is sound going with lavaliers? Go down five points on the Variac. How about a Mole fan or a Ritter? Where's the Ubangi? Trace the 5 K.

The Big Picture

You find yourself linguistically lost in the banter of the set—F.D.R., Count Bassie, sex and travel—and awash in technospeak—HMIs, tungsten, Keno flos, ultra-Dinos. A tourist in a foreign land where everyone seems to be named "Moe," you are left baffled by the seemingly dysphasic, expressive language disorder that is spoken on the set.

Like most other languages, the origin of this one is found, unquestionably, in inherent isolation. Rather than the geographic isolation that is often at the root of language diversity, the language of film production stems from professional isolation. The community of filmmakers is comprised of a self-selected, relatively small population that migrates from project to project and works in close quarters. The result is a sort of linguistic drift from English to movie parlance. It is a language that is built on terse dialogue, acronyms, fabled phrases, movie slang, and profanity: a highly specialized Creole developed not from the endemic, insular intermixing of a European and African language, but one stemming from the collision of the individual vocabularies of sound and camera and electric. Further refined by a coupling of street language and the dialogue of film schools, distorted by the influence of international crews, with their requisite slaughtering of phrases. Crew members who worked with the Czechoslovakian cinematographer Mirsolav Ondrícek knew exactly what he meant when he used the word *chicken* for *kitchen,* or when he said, "Seventy-six the monkey." Not English, not Czech, just a hybrid, colloquial film idiom.

Throw in some terms from the theater, the dialect of acting coaches and studio executives, toss it about with the highly technical and specialized jargon of each department, and we have a whole new language. It is idiomatic and idiosyncratic. Sometimes lacking any type of linguistic form and syntax, the words and phrases typically shortened and pared down. Often

10

uttered in brief unstructured statements lacking the flourishes and patterns of normal speech. The language of the set, more a string of commands, and questions, a collection of simple acronyms, and abbreviated statements of fact. We're in. Take the china ball down five points. M.O.S. Put a double net over all and drop a half single in the deuce. A language and vocabulary built on the strange mutated lexicon of film production.

It is also regional, stemming from the geography separating East and West Coast filmmakers, creating a partial linguistic bifurcation. A splintering of east coast and west coast dialects and phraseology. A vocabulary, passed down from generation to generation and set to set, a byproduct of the oral history of filmmaking on each coast.

At the end of the shooting day, the crew slips into a sparse, almost laconic linguistic pattern, a dialect with a brevity and gruffness rooted in exhaustion, fueled by little more than the spartan hope that soon they will hear the words that announce the "Abby Singer," the second to last shot of the day, and then the fabled, long-awaited words declaring that final shot. Referred to interchangeably as either the martini (West Coast) or the window (East Coast); in the vernacular the L.F.S.—last f—king shot. While blatantly profane, it is aptly descriptive, an acronym that plays out like a long-awaited bugle call heralding the wrap.

But remember that before you get anywhere near the end of a day, and even before you start tripping over the diction of this foreign tongue, if you are a first-time director, the first thing you will hear on the very first day of shooting from the assistant director is the very clear, the very concise, the simple, straightforward English words, "So, what do you want to do?"

They are at once completely comprehendible yet undoubtedly the most baffling words of all. Neither technical nor profane, not abbreviated or slang, yet they stop you in your tracks. Just like a simple phrase spoken to a tourist who knows only pigeon French, the question "So, what do you want to do?" can leave you feeling dumbfounded, your mind rendered blank. It is in that single moment that you know you can't possibly respond in even the most simplistic way until you learn not only the vocabulary of film but the language of the set, as well.

PICK YOUR TEN BEST SHOTS.

LET'S say you're a director about to shoot your first feature film. It's 7:00 A.M. on the first day of a fifty-two day shoot, and you feel like you're standing at the foot of Mount Everest. You wrote the script, raised the cash for the project yourself, planned every detail of this cinematic assault during months of preproduction, and right now you have everything you might need strapped to the back of a yak.

You take a deep breath, look around, and see that you have more equipment than you know what to do with, and that you are surrounded by a crew of filmmaking Sherpas who have all made this climb many times before.

Outfitted in alternating layers of polar fleece and the high-tech impenetrable fabric of near-manic optimism, you make George Mallory's "We will stomp to the top with the wind in our teeth" speech to the crew as you mentally prepare to charge the summit.

Undeterred by the less than overwhelming reaction of the Sherpa crew to your troop-rallying words, it's now seven fifteen and you're still brimming with enthusiasm. You are more than abundantly confidant that you know what is ahead of you. You've anticipated the tough days, the thin air, the Nepalese nights. After all, it's Everest, for God's sake.

But before you scale the Khumbu Icefall or enter the

The Big Picture

Valley of Death, before you can go back to thinking about the Hillary Step or reaching day fifty-two and planting your flag on the summit, you look over and the first assistant director, oddly festooned in the attire of an ordinary day, calmly says that rather than charging the summit, today you must simply trek to the first base camp.

You are geared up, mentally prepared for a rapid assent, more than ready to sink your crampons into sheet ice and climb, and he tells you that you simply need to *walk*. He says, "Just pick your ten best shots and let's make the day's work."

As the wind is sucked out of you, you briefly entertain the possibility that this calm and rational assistant director is wrong, and that he has no idea how big, how Himalayan, your plan actually is. You think, Ten best shots? I was going to do that by noon. He then points vaguely in the direction of the mountainous mass of crew and trucks and starts talking about the law of averages. That, on average, most directors can get ten shots a day. He says that on a typical day shooting an interior, the director will only "get the set" for two hours. That the other nine or ten hours will be spent blocking and lighting. You start to feel the symptoms of altitude sickness even though you are still practically at sea level. You wonder, Did Tenzing Norgay tell Sir Edmund Hillary how far he could climb in a single day?

He looks you straight in the eye and reiterates exactly what he said before: "A good strategy is to pick your 'best ten' so you have a chance of making them." He says that if you want to do much more than that, it will probably look a little sloppy, like TV. You recall the line from *Annie Hall* when Alvy Singer says, "they don't throw their garbage away, they turn it into television," and you feel your legs go weak. You haven't shot a single foot of film and already a death wobble.

You look at him as you stand on the south side of your

14

PICK YOUR TEN BEST SHOTS.

Everest, knowing that less than a third of climbers ever reach the summit and that the odds of a successful feature film are far worse than that. As he continues on about camera setups and the hours needed for makeup and hair, you remember that he's worked side by side with the demigods, the supreme beings of the cinematic cosmos: Woody Allen, Sydney Pollack, Taylor Hackford, Irwin Winkler, Alfonso Cuarón. . . . Reluctantly, you accept the fact that films and mountains are scaled one shot, and one step, at a time. Then you put down your ice ax and simply begin to walk.

You make a shot list for the day. You pick your "best ten" because that guy over there, that yogurt-eating, yak-riding Sherpa of an AD who has scaled this mountain, day in and day out for years, says that that is how you climb to the highest point on Earth. Ten shots at a time.

WHAT IS A SHOT, ANYWAY?

IN order for a director to decide how to cover a scene, he first has to block it—that is, determine where the actors will be and what they will be doing. From there, the director and DP have to decide where the camera will be for the first shot (generally a master shot of the entire scene). All covering shots are then determined based on the master. While a scene can be either covered in a single shot or constructed from a series of shots, a "shot" is what is filmed in a single camera setup.

A single shot can be as simple as an insert (say a close-up of a newspaper) or an establishing shot (a wide shot of a house) or as complex as a moving master (an entire scene covered in a single, often intricate shot). As a result, there is not a simple, linear, mathematical translation of shot to screen time. A shot may be anywhere from several seconds to ten minutes in length. (A shot, under normal circumstances, is not longer than ten minutes for the simple reason that a film magazine holds only one thousand feet, or ten minutes of film.) But long or short, simple or complex, a shot is merely what is photographed in between the words *action* and *cut*.

For an action sequence, a director may choose to build the energy in a scene through a series of quick cuts, where a shot may require only six or twelve frames. Since there are twenty-four frames per second, that's only a fraction of a second of screen time. In this case, a series of shots would be needed to cut together in order to construct a scene. For an action sequence in *Rollerball*, director John McTiernan ("McT") needed a shot of a stuntman flying off of a motorcycle to cut into a longer sequence. With the camera on the floor at a low angle, and the motorcycle and stuntman on scaffolding about ten feet up and in front of a green screen, the stuntman flipped the bike over and fell ten feet to pads on the floor. McT knew that ultimately, when the film was cut together, he needed only a quarter- or a half-second piece of film of that motorcycle rider flying through the air. He equated directing to engineering; building something complex out of a lot of small pieces.

Yet a single shot can also be much longer and far more complicated. It can be a lengthy moving master with a series of sophisticated camera moves. It can involve dollies, cranes, zooms, and pans. It can utilize elaborate lighting and choreography, not only for the actors and dialogue but for the camera moves, as well. An entire scene can be covered in a single lengthy shot where the actors and the camera move, or with a tied-off camera and stationary actors, or anything in between.

Woody shot a ten-minute moving master in one continuous take for *Mighty Aphrodite*. We follow Lenny (played by Woody) and Linda Ash (played by Mira Sorvino) as they move through her apartment in a series of singles (one actor in frame) and two shots (two actors in frame.) As it was being shot, the actors moved in and out of frame and delivered their lines all in a single take. One shot, ten minutes long. (In the released version, the scene runs just over seven minutes, with three cutaways.) In this case, the fast pacing, energy, and comedy are created by performance and shot design, not editing. Note that this shot, originally ten minutes in length, was roughly 10 percent of the screenplay, filmed in just a few hours. Due to the complex blocking and lighting, the actors and the camera operator had to be able to hit their marks, execute the camera moves, and deliver the dialogue flawlessly.

A scene that is covered with a lot of different angles is constructed in the editing room, where it is cut together from pieces of all of the shots. The motion and drama of the scene enhanced by editing techniques.

Yet a scene that is covered in a single shot is constructed on the set. The drama and suspense built into it by innovative shot design, by riveting acting, and by well-executed camera moves and lighting; not by editing.

When you are scheduling a film, you may not know whether the director will decide to cover the scene in a single master shot or by using standard coverage (a master, close-ups over the shoulders, reverses, etc.). A single master will take a significant amount of time to block, rehearse, and light. In a complex shot, the actors have to learn their movement and line timing and the camera operator has to learn the camera moves. On the other hand, shooting a scene with more standard coverage will usually take even more time as you move the equipment and relight for each camera setup.

Many directors, including Woody, don't know how they will cover a scene until the day of shooting. When they stand on the set, when they consider the dynamics of the connecting scenes, when they look at the day's work set before them and what they want artistically from the scheduled scene, when they see how much time and what equipment they have at their disposal, they make a shot list for the day. Yet the day has already been scheduled, probably two months beforehand, based on experience and the law of averages. When all is said and done, no matter how the scene is covered, generally speaking, plan on shooting 2⅛ pages a day, which translates to two and a half minutes of master time, and know that most directors will be able to get ten shots in a day.

5

IF IT'S NOT IN THE SHOT, IT DOESN'T MATTER.

TRY to imagine one of your favorite scenes in a film. It doesn't matter if it's a love scene or a suspense-filled cliff-hanger, a fast-paced sequence from an action film or a compelling dramatic piece. Just think about how completely caught up in that moment you were when you first saw it up on the screen. Then consider that standing a couple of feet away at that great dramatic moment, that couple tangled up in the sheets or that kid clinging to the cliff, was a film crew and several tons of equipment. And that most of the real passion, the real cliff-hanging moments occurred in the drama behind the camera, not in the acting in front of it.

Yet just like the film viewer, the filmmaker has to take everything that is not in the current shot and let it go. Because filmmaking, like film viewing, works only if you believe that what is between the frame lines of the shot in front of you is the only thing that matters at the moment. Films are made and watched one very focused shot at a time. The director has to be able to mentally and emotionally divert everything from his mind except whatever is in the shot that he is filming "right now." To allow himself to become as tangled up in the shot as the actors in front of the camera are tangled up in the sheets, and as tangled up as he hopes the viewer of the film will be, "in the moment."

In filmmaking, there is an argument, if not an imperative,

for staying focused. There are an infinite number of distractions and an ever-growing list of competing variables, many of which are beyond your control and all of which can fuel insecurity and self-doubt. There are numerous departments with conflicting and interdependent needs, and the constant requisite to determine what to do right now for the current shot, but also to make decisions regarding each subsequent shot and each subsequent shooting day as issues arise. A virtual sandstorm of information is swirling around the set, and all those unretractable, hard decisions represent financial and creative commitments that are often made on the fly. The director stands at the vortex of these distractions, and stress levels can run enormously high. Often so much so, that it can be debilitating.

As a director, you may be standing on the set, trying to think about how to block a scene, when you find out that not only has the actress you wanted to play an important supporting role turned you down but so have your second and third choices for the part. Since her first scene plays next week, you have to cast someone immediately. But before you begin to think about who else might work for the part, you hear that the director of photography just got a lab report on dailies and there was a flare in the lens for all three prints of last night's close-up. Then your personal assistant delivers a message that the studio wants a conference call this afternoon. That they may be "sending somebody out" for a few days to be on set. The knot in your stomach tightens.

You are reminded that one of the actresses has decided she wants to wear a wig instead of having to deal with her own hair. You are told that will cost six thousand dollars that is not in the budget. Furthermore, she is insisting that she be a blonde, not a brunette, as you had planned.

As this information flows in from each department you try to remain objective, but still your blood pressure ticks up.

IF IT'S NOT IN THE SHOT, IT DOESN'T MATTER.

That magnificent apartment you had hoped to shoot in has just fallen through. The co-op board doesn't want to deal with the liability. No room for negotiation. The location department is on it, but you can forget Block Island for the weekend, since you'll be scouting both days. The apartment has to work in ten days, because the actress you cast to work in those scenes is starting a play in London the following week. She has been guaranteed $500,000, and unlike your weekend, she has a "pay or play" deal.

As you slug down some lukewarm coffee, further spiking your adrenaline—exactly what you don't need—the AD says, "Ten-minute warning." The set will be lit and the cast ready to go (you, too) ten minutes from now.

Still time for more news, though. A note from the producer: even though you hear a lot of jazz in the sound track, the studio REALLY wants to lay in some rap music. They, of course, have just the guy to do it, because they're shooting a film with him right after yours. The producer in New York says he'll start fighting the battle as soon as they drift into their offices on the coast in three hours.

You glance at your BlackBerry. Thirty-three new messages. You still have six minutes to scroll.

The stunt coordinator is having trouble finding a double for your leading man, who can do "high work" (walk on steel girders eighty stories over the street). Casting wants you for a half hour—anytime. The animal trainer has a great mastiff but no Dobermans. Is that okay?

Shooting on the Brooklyn Bridge is fine, but it must be a week from Sunday. There goes your ten-year-old's birthday party. The long-range forecast for next week is heavy rain, but you have cover for only two days. Can another scene be rewritten or moved somewhere—anywhere—else?

You reach for your Tums.

The Big Picture

You are given a five-minute warning as a production assistant bounds up with a message from your wife. It reads: "Don't get upset. Everyone is fine, but your teenage daughter backed her car into a garbage truck. It may be totaled." As you contemplate the replacement cost of the car, you want to scream at someone, but all you see is the flushed and smiling face of the PA. You remind yourself that you can't kill the messenger.

The AD comes up and informs you, "We're set to go. First teams coming in." And then asks, "Is everything okay?" You just look at him. "Don't worry," he says, "seven months from now, you'll be standing at the crew screening. We'll get there. For now, let's just get this shot . . ."

The leading lady walks onto the set and smiles. You walk over to give her a hug and tell her how great she looks. You try to block everything else out.

As the camera rolls, you lose your best take because a bus drives by and wipes out the sound. The sun slips behind a cloud and costs you ten minutes. Your leading man has always hated this scene and you know he's going to torture you. As the cast reassembles, the AD whispers that the generator is down, they're switching to a new machine and that'll be another twenty minutes. Though the blood is pounding in your temples, he seems oddly poised, almost smiling. "Relax," he says. "We've anticipated all this. We'll make the day's work. Just concentrate on the shot. For now, the rest doesn't matter . . ."

6

STORIES DON'T HAVE TO BE LINEAR. CONSIDER CREATIVE WAYS TO WARP TIME.

THERE are lots of obvious ways to introduce a time lapse within a film. The most simplistic and straightforward include graphics, like a "Two Weeks Earlier" or "One Year Later" tag on the bottom of the screen, or cutting away to an establishing shot of the sun rising on a new day. For a longer lapse, the director may choose to introduce a change of season or use makeup techniques to age the actors. For a more extended time change, a different actor can be cast to play the younger or older version of a character, as in Lajos Koltai's *Evening,* where Mamie Gummer, Meryl Streep's daughter in real life, plays the younger version of Meryl's character in the film, or Woody's frequent use of a skinny redheaded ten-year-old to play his younger self in films like *Annie Hall* and *Radio Days.*

Regardless of whether the time lapse is a flashback or a flash-forward, short or long, there are a number of possible ways to communicate a time passage in a film. But before you reflexively select one of the tried-and-true or pedestrian techniques of an on screen "time jump," it is worth considering that there are far more sophisticated and engaging ways to move around in time and space within a film. By employing more complex cinematic techniques both to propel the story and transport the viewer in time, you can capitalize on creative elements unique to the art of film, like shot composition, set design, and editing, and use them to your creative advantage while giving the film some intellectual depth.

In analyzing the film *Stardust Memories,* there are a number of time jumps, back and forth, from present time to the distant and more recent past, that are accomplished in creative and unique ways. Beginning with the film within the film, we jump from inside one of Sandy Bates's movies to the screening room where it is being viewed, then later, back and forth again, into and out of the film and the film set. While this may not be conceived as a traditional passage of time, it certainly represents a transition from one location in time to another, since Woody plays the lead in both the film and the film within the film. But this is only the beginning of the time shifts in *Stardust Memories.*

Consider the scene we called "The Elephant on the Beach," in which the character of Sandy Bates, played by Woody, steps into, and out of, a memory that encompasses an extended leap in time. As the scene is established, we hold on the starry-eyed, off-in-the-distance gaze of Sandy Bates as he sits in a restaurant and looks out at the beach. This cinematic pause is our initial hint that we may be headed someplace else. We then cut from Sandy's point of view to a two shot of the young Sandy and the woman who we assume to be his mother on the beach. From Woody's reminiscent look, and the fact that the child was established earlier as his younger self, we know this is a memory, or flashback. So far, pretty basic. But then the shot gets really interesting. The ten-year-old Sandy, hoping for a birthday wish too childishly fantastic to ever be actually granted—an elephant—runs out of frame and the thirty-year-old Sandy steps back in. This transports the scene not only through time and into the arena of a memory but into the realm of fantasy, as well. The scene progresses, taking us from Sandy's childhood memory to the current time, where the older Sandy and his girlfriend, Dorrie, played by Charlotte Rampling, stand in the same spot on the beach, engaged in the same activity—exchanging a birthday gift—thus completing the scene twenty years later without a graphic in sight or a cut in the sequence. Within the confines of this scene, representing just a few minutes of screen time, we cover a lot of territory. Traveling from present day to both the subconscious and back in time twenty years, then back to the present. The entire transition communicated through brilliant writing and directing, innovative shot construction, and inspired cinematography.

A second novel device for warping time occurs in *Stardust Memories* with the ingenious use of set design as a vehicle for denoting a transition in time as well as a shift in the psychological mind-set of a character. Look at the first scene played in Sandy's apartment. The viewer is presented with him standing in front of, and literally dwarfed by, a large blowup of Eddie Adams's internationally acclaimed photo of Nguyen Van Lem, a Vietcong operative frozen on film at the moment of his death—the gun still pointed to his head. The photo is dramatic in both size and content, demonstrating Sandy Bates's state of mind while subtly establishing a time frame. Without any other change, a later scene transports us back in time and depicts Sandy's sunnier mental state when a scene is played in exactly the same spot, but the photo is now of a smiling Groucho Marx. Woody uses this device and alters the photo twice more in the film to denote an instantaneous and unequivocal shift in time and mental state and accomplishes it with a dramatic change in the "wall paper."

Woody, in collaboration with production designer Mel Bourne, used this element of set design to help flesh out and define the character, establish a time line, drive the plot, and deliver a comedic jab. The sheer size of the photograph and how it towers over the character of Sandy Bates is a strong visual depiction of how his mind-set dominates both his art and his life, and seamlessly telegraphs a time warp within the film, as well. It is definitive. It is intelligent. It is humorous, and it is visually compelling. From a filmmaking standpoint, it is exceptionally well crafted and it is certainly anything but pedestrian.

The bottom line? Sure, you can resort to the in-your-face hit 'em over the head, no possible confusion of a graphic on the bottom of the screen, or you can be inventive and exploit the full breadth of possibilities available to you as a filmmaker. Think groundbreaking shot design, inspired set decoration, provocative writing and editing, and leave the graphics for cereal boxes and television. Warp time in a creative way.

7

DON'T LEAVE MONEY ON THE
EDITING ROOM FLOOR. SIZE MATTERS.

FILMMAKING, in many ways, is like construction and the script is the architectural blueprint for a film. To my knowledge, contractors don't often build homes with extra rooms only to tear them down after they are finished because the house is too big for the lot. It's obvious to everyone that this would be an enormous waste of money. Yet in filmmaking, it is not uncommon to do just that. And those metaphorically lopped-off rooms, those cut scenes lying on the editing room floor, cost a lot of money to shoot. In many cases, much more money than any builder might spend on a few extra rooms for a house. So how does this happen? Quite simply, the studios often sign off on scripts that are just too long.

Which brings me to size. In a script at least, it matters. And it matters to the tune of tens of thousands of dollars for each extra page. And here again, Woody gets it right. In the case of scripts, bigger is not better. On the eighteen films of his that I worked on, virtually all of the scripts ran from ninety to one hundred pages. No extra rooms here. And it's not because he is short of words. He just knows that if he writes a script any longer than that, he may end up cutting scenes out. Obviously, it is easier and cheaper to leave them out of the script than it is to cut them out of the finished film in the editing room.

The Big Picture

Here's how the math breaks down. In general when timing a script, you can figure about a minute of screen time per page of dialogue. The script for *Stardust Memories* was ninety-five pages, which resulted in a running time of roughly eighty-eight minutes. A perfect length for a comedy. If we, on average, shoot 2⅝ pages a day on a feature film, to shoot an extra twenty-five pages will take an additional ten days. At an average of $150,000 dollars a day, to shoot that extra ink will cost in the ballpark of $1.5 million.

Now back to my analogy about building a house. Let's say you do shoot that 125-page script. You now have a Mc-Mansion of a movie. With a running time of two hours and five minutes, your rough cut may feel a little too long. It may seem a little slow at times. The pacing is off. It's dragging. So what do you do? The simple answer? More editing to shorten and tighten.

But before you start snipping, you have to consider how removing scenes will affect the story line. Will removing a few scenes leave any missed story points or "empty hallways" leading nowhere? Will you have to go back and reshoot some new scenes to tie things together? (Yet another expense to add in.) Then, consider this: If you can cut out twenty-five pages, or twenty-five minutes, from a finished film and the story still works, how important were those pages anyway?

After you do decide which scenes you can do without and you're done cutting, look down at the editing room floor and there, in bits and pieces of celluloid, are roughly ten shooting days, or $1.5 million. And your movie is back to where it should have been before you started shooting it; the very livable size of one hundred pages. Just before you sweep up and toss those scenes away or drag them into the trash bin on your computer, take a minute or two and consider what you could have done with that extra $1.5 million back when you were shooting those scenes.

DON'T LEAVE MONEY ON THE EDITING ROOM FLOOR.

Obviously, I'm working with a lot of averages here. Many movies are longer than 140 minutes, and should be—*Lawrence of Arabia, Spider Man,* and *Titanic,* to name a few. Also, shooting dialogue between two actors in a kitchen will go faster and cost less than shooting a scene that reads "The invasion of Normandy Beach," 1/8 page. But the point is, always do the math. Go lean. Don't rely on "dump-truck editing"—Especially on that student or indie film you're financing with a credit card. Tighten up the script. Understand that page count matters. It's the first thing I check when I receive a script to read. In general, use the hundred-page rule and make sure you don't leave money on the editing room floor. When writing a script, size matters.

8

DON'T UNDERESTIMATE THE POWER OF A SINGLE LINE.

WE all know them. Those movie lines that are so singularly powerful that they take on iconic status. From Rhett Butler's classic declaration in *Gone with the Wind*—"Frankly, my dear, I don't give a damn," to Dorothy's statement of the obvious in *The Wizard of Oz,* ". . . we're not in Kansas anymore." From Tom Hanks's chilling delivery of the words "Houston, we have a problem," in *Apollo 13* to the riveting force of Jack Nicholson's statement in *A Few Good Men,* "You can't handle the truth!" These lines resonate with such force with the audience that they take on a life beyond the big screen, carrying meaning even when removed from the context of the movie. Like every other element of a film, these lines began with the script and the writing, yet it is the collaborative art of filmmaking, everything from the performance of those words to how they are captured on film, that allows them to have the impact, the blunt force and momentum to seep out of the theater and become part of the vernacular, the language of our popular culture.

Consider the almost Pavlovian expectation built around Arnold Schwarzenegger's infamous declarations "I'll be back" and "Hasta la vista, baby," or Clint Eastwood's "Go ahead, make my day." Or consider the romantic musing from *Casablanca,* "We'll always have Paris," and from *Jerry Maguire,* "You had me at 'hello.'" For these powerful lines to become powerful moments that can define a film, they have to be crafted for the screen. The director has to capture a performance with the tone and inflection, the pacing and force that these words command. From casting choices and shot selection to how the scenes are covered and lit, these words are given depth and longevity. It is ultimately the translation of these words into the language of film that empowers them.

Yet there are so many truly great films that don't have a single stand-alone line. Try to remember a quote from your own self-defined list of great films. Or pick from the list of compelling, significant, critically acclaimed films like *Twelve Angry Men, Dr. Strangelove, The Bridge on the River Kwai, Traffic, Crash, Hotel Rwanda,* or *Interiors* and try to recall a significant line from one of them. You probably can't.

Why? Because in some films, no single line is memorable, but every line matters. Some films are simply about *all* the writing. So don't discount the importance of a single line, not only because one of them could become imbedded in the lexicon of pop culture but also because, in a truly great film, the sum total of all the lines is ultimately what matters. A film begins with the written word.

9

MOVE THE WALLS, NOT THE TRUCKS. BUILDING A SET GIVES YOU TOTAL CONTROL.

SIMPLE fact: While films can be shot entirely on built sets at a studio, or completely at practical locations, most films are shot on a combination of both. How do we decide when to find a location, or when to build it? Should we fly to the Everglades and shoot if the script calls for it, or should we re-create or "build" the Everglades on a stage? How about a scene on the beach, or in an apartment? Or at F. A. O. Schwarz or Coney Island? Is it better from an artistic standpoint to shoot it practically on location, or duplicate it in a studio? Which will look better on screen? What is the cost differential and the impact on the schedule? Are there any logistical barriers or safety concerns? Now multiply these dynamics by every scene in the movie. Taking into account that there may be, on average, fifty different locations in a film, how do we decide when to build and when to hit the streets?

When making these decisions, there are some rules of thumb. First, many locations are impossible to shoot live— outer space, for example, or the White House, or many co-op buildings in Manhattan. (The co-op boards just won't allow it.) So that makes it easy. If the script calls for a location that we can't get—say the interior of the Sistine Chapel or a space shuttle, we will have to build it.

But assuming that we do have a choice, we have to consider the pros and cons of each. For example, building gives us more control and allows us to move faster. Generally, we can expect to shoot three pages of dialogue a day on a built set in a studio, and only two and a half pages a day at a live location. So if we build our sets we can, on average, gain a half a page a day, or roughly one full shooting day per week. If the shooting day is running $150,000, this adds up quickly.

What are the factors that allow us to move faster on a built set? For starters, once we load into the studio, we're there for the duration. No need to travel or haul equipment in and out. We also move faster in the studio because built sets are designed and constructed with features that facilitate filming. No ceilings for example, which provides a structural asset that allows us to easily mount overhead lights. The construction crews also build walls that can be "pulled" to permit more diverse camera angles and provide greater creative flexibility, as well as easy access for equipment and electrical cabling. Built sets can be easily pre-rigged for lighting, saving an enormous amount of time when we arrive with a full crew to shoot. On a built set, we are also not hampered by weather, pedestrians, traffic, noise, location-mandated time constraints, and many other, often unforeseen elements that inevitably materialize when we shoot at a live location.

You may think, Well, if you have a choice, why not build everything? It's faster and cheaper, and allows for greater creative flexibility. . . .

But it's never that simple.

While building a set contains the production and provides a greater degree of control, shooting at a live location often opens a scene up. Consider two scenes, both of which involve a couple of people on a beach; Harrison Ford and Julia Ormond in *Sabrina* and Nick Nolte and Blythe Danner in *The Prince of Tides*. Both call for two people interacting on a beach at night, yet one we built on a stage in New York and the other we shot live on Fripp Island in South Carolina.

Although we flew to Martha's Vineyard on *Sabrina* to shoot some practical locations—houses, streets, et cetera—director Sydney Pollack chose to shoot the picnic on the beach on a stage in New York so we could control the environment. We actually built ourselves a little corner of Martha's Vineyard at Kaufman Astoria Studios in Queens. We brought in twenty tons of sand, a dune fence, built a rickety pier and a gas-fueled fire pit, and we had ourselves a beach. No pounding ocean waves, no wind blowing Julia's hair or drowning out the dialogue. The DP, the great Giuseppe Rotunno (cinematographer on nine films with Federico Fellini), was able to manipulate the amount of light in the night sky and the size of the flame in the fire pit quite easily inside the studio. We didn't have to wait for the sun to set or the tide to shift. We could shoot our night scene during the day, leaving the crew and the actors fresh and the schedule simplified. Building on the stage was cost-effective and it worked artistically for the scene because the picnic was shot in intimate close-ups. For this scene, Sydney didn't need a wide shot of the beach. We moved the walls, not the trucks. Building a set gave us total control.

Yet for Barbra Streisand's *The Prince of Tides,* we headed out to the beach on Fripp Island, near Beaufort, South Carolina, with truckloads of equipment and a full crew. I had to monitor the weather, study tide charts, and deal with the fluid nature of wind, water, sand, and light. In this particular scene, the character of Tom Wingo, played by Nick Nolte, sprints across the sand along the water's edge in anger and frustration after a confrontation with his wife, played by Blythe Danner. Since Barbra wanted a wide, expansive shot of the beach, the aesthetic requirements of the script made the decision for us. It was simply too much to build on a stage. The truth is, we can build a small corner of the beach, but not the whole thing.

MOVE THE WALLS, NOT THE TRUCKS.

Yet the decision to build a set, or to travel to a location, is affected by more than the size of the lens on the camera and the scope of the scene. On the film *Just Cause,* the script called for a number of scenes to be shot in the Florida Everglades. Some of these scenes required a wide lens to showcase the beauty and expanse of the Everglades in the daylight, so we shot these scenes at a live location. The shooting crew went to a makeshift "alligator boot camp" to learn about the swamp. It was no comfort to hear that alligators can run faster than a man, or that it was mating season and they were particularly aggressive and prone to lurking in the drainpipes.

Even though we took every precaution, there were still significant risks working in such an environment. On the shoot, we had three armed alligator wranglers with us at all times. Since alligators are a protected species, the wranglers went in before the call to humanely and temporarily remove as many of them as they could from the area where we would be filming. But it quickly became clear that there was no way we could safely shoot the night work on location. The dynamics of the Everglades shift when the sun sets. It was far too dangerous to send the cast and crew into this environment with the poor visibility offered at night. But the dark of night mandated by the script also meant we didn't need to see much background. So for the night work, we re-created a section of the Everglades with pools of water two feet deep and thousands of trees on a stage the size of a high school gymnasium.

You might ask, If you went to the effort and cost of building the Everglades, why didn't you just shoot the whole sequence on the stage? Simple. We couldn't build enough of the Everglades for the wide daytime shots to work. But under the cover of darkness, the built set filled the bill. We shot the Everglades live *and* we built it on a stage. In so doing, we met the artistic needs of the film and the practical safety issues of the location, as well.

The Big Picture

But these examples are all of exterior locations. What about interiors? Plenty of scenes are shot at locations that don't offer either wide-open vistas or life-threatening reptiles. How about apartments, offices, restaurants? Why not just build all interiors?

So far, we have managed to ignore the more straightforward issue of the budget. What is the cost differential between building a set on a stage and "buying" that live location? If we build, there are construction costs, but we can move faster. If we shoot on location, we must rent that location for the time that we are there and we lose roughly half a page a day.

The math gets interesting, in part because what we are building doesn't have great structural demands. For example, when we build a set on a stage, there is no foundation, no insulation, plumbing, wiring, or ceiling. Walls are often built with lightweight wood backed by bracing, not two-by-fours and Sheetrock. Anything not in the shot—say the exterior of a house—isn't built at all, and anything that can be "cheated," is. The marble columns for the United States Supreme Court set in Rod Lurie's *Nothing But the Truth* were made from cardboard cylinders and faux, trompe l'oeil, marbleized paint. As a result, building costs, which can vary greatly depending on what is being constructed, run eighty to one hundred dollars per square foot, compared to standard building costs, which can run three to five times that.

While each set and each film is different, there is a rule of thumb that if we are going to shoot at a location for more than three days, it may be economically feasible to consider building it. On the other hand, if we have less than three days—say just a few pages of dialogue—it's probably not worth the cost of building. We can undoubtedly find a location in the real world that will work artistically and cost less than building a set, even after factoring in the lost half page.

It starts to become apparent why some scenes are shot

on built sets and some on practical locations. The built set at the studio is more contained. No pedestrians. No alligators. No tides or unscheduled gusts of wind. Fewer surprises. No travel time. A built set provides easy access to everything we need and offers us speed, flexibility, and the opportunity for innovative shots. For this reason, we built an entire nineteenth-century Eastern European city the size of a football field (designed by Santo Loquasto) on a stage for *Shadows and Fog*. The film, brilliantly photographed by Carlo Di Palma in the style of German Expressionist films, with exaggerated and symbolic use of light and shadow, arresting architectural structures, and circular shots, would have been extraordinarily difficult to execute as well if we had shot it completely at night and on location.

But consider that there are places with extraordinary production value—say that ancient amphitheater we shot at in Taormina, Sicily, for *Mighty Aphrodite,* the streets of Paris for *Sabrina,* Central Park, St. Patrick's Cathedral, the Low Country of South Carolina, or the boardwalk at the Jersey shore— that would simply be too costly or not feasible to re-create on a stage and that should be shot live. Then consider that for *A Midsummer Night's Sex Comedy,* we got the best of both worlds when we built a turn-of-the-century farmhouse and then brought it to a location so the interiors *and* exteriors could be tied together.

As filmmakers, shooting live locations offers us a patchwork of stitched-together days: a street corner in the morning, an apartment in the afternoon, two days at an office across town. We keep the trucks and the crew moving. There is travel time between each location, the load-in and load-out of equipment. With each move, the camera's not running as the clock slowly consumes the shooting day. Each new location presents both obstacles and advantages. The production value of the architecture and authenticity offered by Grand Central

The Big Picture

Terminal, offset by the logistics of dealing with the crowds, the restricted hours, the noise. Throw in some live trains, the third rail, the fluid, frenetic pace of rush hours. And while it may be faster, cheaper, and in many ways easier to build our sets and shoot everything in the studio, remember that shooting on location offers a great deal of aesthetic value. In so doing, we capture both the grandeur and the patina, the unparalleled appeal and grit of New York, the architecture of Paris, or the feel of the South Carolina Low Country in a way that would be impossible to do on a stage.

But don't forget the financial component, or the three-day rule, or the production value of a wide-open beach. And don't forget that while Hollywood has its back lots, only New York has New York. And that it is on the shoulders of this city, on her avenues and behind her doors, in her neighborhoods and on her faces, that East Coast filmmaking is borne. Think back to the rich history of modern New York cinema. Begin in 1954 with the eight Oscars awarded to Elia Kazan's *On The Waterfront.* Then think Woody Allen's *Annie Hall, Hannah and Her Sisters,* and *Broadway Danny Rose,* or Martin Scorsese's *Mean Streets, Taxi Driver,* and *Raging Bull.* Think Sidney Lumet and *Serpico, Network,* and *Dog Day Afternoon.*

So move the walls, not the trucks. Go ahead and build that office, that apartment, that corner of the beach. But then get it real, and get it right and find some locations on the streets.

10

KNOW YOUR WAY AROUND THE MARKETPLACE AS WELL AS THE PALACE.

MY very first film as a Directors Guild trainee in 1978 was Philip Kaufman's *The Wanderers*. A really tough project about the 1960s and the street gangs of the Bronx. The real-life stories of the Fordham Baldies, the Ducky Boys, and the Golden Guineas—a sort of *West Side Story,* just farther north.

I had never spent much time in New York prior to this, and found the decaying, burned-out neighborhoods of the South Bronx, with the requisite dead dogs, rotting stench, and drug dealers, a harsh introduction to this city and about as far removed from my perception of the glamour of the movie business as you could get. The welcome mat of a night shoot, a fire in a trash can, and random gunfire fueled my inclination to run for cover and completely overshadowed both New York and new job. Most of the time, I was too concerned for my life to care much about the neighborhoods south of Fordham Road.

The year before I arrived in New York, in 1977, NASA sent out the twin *Voyager* spacecrafts, space and time capsules with a recording of greetings in fifty-five different languages, in the hopes of making contact with extraterrestrial life. Both spacecrafts containing a gold-plated record with some "murmurs from the Earth."

I remember thinking at the time that there were close to

seven thousand languages known to be spoken in the world. In Papua New Guinea alone there were 820, all of them indigenous, yet NASA thought they might get a hit with one of the fifty-five. That some life-form in another galaxy might be able to decipher Sumerian or Sotho.

Walking quickly through the streets near Fordham Road in the Bronx, mostly late at night or at sunrise, when the only people out were the very down-and-out or, odd as it may seem, those earning a studio paycheck, I would have sworn that there were far more than 820 languages being spoken in just a single block of the Bronx. That the streets around Fordham Road and Valentine Avenue surely must top New Guinea, if not in indigenous, then at least in the category of immigrant languages. Or if not in languages, then in dialects. Those linguistic offshoots and mutations aptly defined as "an unimportant tongue lacking official status."

Which brings me back to Fordham Road and my introduction to the dialect of the street. A dialect that, due to the circumstances of a particularly tough night, I dubbed "Stoop." Stoop, a succinct pattern of speech, short and to the point. Introduced to me by the phrase, "get the f—k off my stoop or I'll shoot you." It was a real Marie Antoinette meets Betty Crocker—"Let them eat cake"—moment for me as I was held hostage by a chunk of cement and left to contemplate the firepower behind this "unimportant tongue."

We were hoping to put a light on a certain set of concrete steps, the self-proclaimed owner of which had neither a signed deal with the location manager nor a permit for the gun he was toting. Or for that matter, skills in the subtle art of diplomacy.

Stoop, as I call it, is a regional dialect, or, more accurately, a sociolect: a dialect of a specific social class. Over the last thirty years shooting in New York's most derelict neighborhoods, I have become quite fluent in Stoop. It is a dialect that you pick up very quickly if you have tendencies toward self-preservation, and one that responds well to both respect and payments in cash.

I must admit that I vastly prefer Stoop to the other dialect I learned since coming to work in the film business. This is also a sociolect, which I call "Studio." (Think private jet, Hermès scarf, BlackBerry, no socks.) New York "street" doesn't translate very well to West Coast "office." Since people in Hollywood rarely speak the sociolect of the cement steps, a statement like "Get the f—k off my stoop or I'll shoot you" is not well understood. The response is usually, something like, "Did you tell him we are shooting a movie?" At which point you put down the phone and look over at the live set, at the streets even the cops tell you they won't go down, and you wish that somehow you could describe the stench of this little corner of the world, or the look in the eyes of the crowned king of the concrete steps to that guy in the cashmere sweater vest on the West Coast. You are certain that if he could just smell what you smell, he might better appreciate the very direct dialect of Stoop.

You try a rough translation of Stoop to Studio when you say, "One of the locations is holding us up for more money," and Cashmere Sweater-vest, No Socks now instantly understands. "Well, just buy him out. Offer him cash. How much could he want? What could that piece of real estate possibly be worth?"

You know that that stoop is worth all the world to that guy in the South Bronx. It is all that he has. A couple of concrete steps. Yet Marie Antoinette, eating *gâteau au chocolat* on the West Coast, can't possibly understand that.

But because money is the universal language and currency of both Stoop and Studio, you trudge back to the stoop with studio's offer of cash and you buy yourself a couple of

The Big Picture

very expensive concrete steps. All the time wondering about bulletproof vests and whether or not NASA, even for a moment, considered putting "Get the f—k off my stoop or I'll shoot you," a murmur from the South Bronx, on the recording for the *Voyager* spacecrafts. Because somebody, somewhere, should plate that in gold.

So learn your way around both the South Bronx and the Hollywood Hills, around the seven thousand languages, the immigrant and the indigenous, the dialects of concrete steps and of cashmere sweater vests. Learn your way around the marketplace as well as the palace, because "We're making a movie here" doesn't mean much if all a person has in the world is the dialect of the streets and the chipped concrete beneath his feet.

11

GREAT CINEMATOGRAPHERS ARE WORTH THEIR WEIGHT IN GOLD.

THE director of photography is, of course, an expert in the nuance and mechanics of the equipment and techniques of film photography, from cameras and lenses to lighting, blocking, shot composition, film emulsions, and filters. So, from a strictly practical perspective, a great DP is worth his weight in gold because of his technical expertise and ability to address the day to-day photographic needs of a film with practical knowledge.

However, from an artistic standpoint, the director of photography is worth his weight in gold because he is integral in defining the cinematic style of a film. A great DP is not only a master technician but also an artist in his own right, who plays a leading role in creating the look the director ultimately gets on the screen. A great DP will be recognized not solely for innovative shot design and sophisticated lighting techniques but also for the way these two elements come together and help define the film as a work of art. Since DPs all have their own unique artistic preferences and styles, and, not insignificantly, degrees of training, experience, and ability, the selection of a director of photography for a film project has far-reaching consequences.

It is important to note that the personal style of the cinematographer affects not only the look of the film but the process of filmmaking, as well. A DP who can block and light a

43

scene fast, and who can design shots in inventive and economical ways that enhance the look of the film, has a direct and immediate impact on the schedule and budget. But even though the speed with which the cinematographer can light has a huge impact on how fast we can do the day's work, it is the cinematographer's contribution from an artistic standpoint that ultimately matters.

Many people don't understand that the director of photography does not actually operate the camera. Under the direction of the DP, a separate and highly trained camera crew, which includes an operator and two camera assistants, does that. Instead, the director of photography works with the film's director to craft the look of the film. He or she has to understand the director's vision for the project as a whole, as well as for each individual scene, then work in consort with the director and key department heads—set design, wardrobe, makeup, et cetera—to execute it.

In the collaborative art of filmmaking it is impossible to completely separate out the contributions of the director of photography from those of the director of the film, especially if you are considering the work of world-class artists like Gordon Willis, Carlo Di Palma, or Sven Nykvist, to name a few. Unquestionably, the film director is responsible for the totality of the film, and certain arenas, like casting and performance, the director owns completely. But when you look at the actual photography, the shot selection, the lighting, the way the camera moves, it is harder to pull apart the interwoven threads of the partnership between cinematographer and director.

If you consider just a single element of a film's photographic style—say camera movement or lighting—and look at the body of work of different cinematographers, you begin to see how critical the right pairing of director and DP and film project can be. For example, a director, when thinking about the look he wants for a film, has to consider how much movement he wants on the screen and how he wants to accomplish it. Consider that you can get movement on-screen in three basic ways. First, by literally moving the camera as you follow the actor's movement within a scene. Second, by creating the illusion of motion, either through editing—by cutting back and forth within a scene—or by using a zoom lens. And third, you can create motion on-screen by moving the actors within the frame lines of a stationary camera. While all cinematographers have their own preferences and styles of shooting, different DPs simply move the camera differently.

If we consider that directors have preferred shooting styles, that DPs have styles they prefer, and that each individual film must find and define its own style, the artistic equation gets complicated. Is the film dramatic? A comedy? A fast-paced action piece? What emotion is the director trying to convey? What stylistic vision does the director have for the film and who would be best suited to shoot it? At first blush, one might assume that suspense or fear may be better accomplished with quick cuts, while a drama or comedy may be better served with less coverage. But then, maybe not. Do quick cuts deliver shock value in a thriller? Of course. But then take a look at the suspense-building Steadicam shots in *The Shining,* with Danny, the little boy, riding the bike down the long hallways of the desolate Overlook Hotel, before you decide that the only way to build fear is with a dramatic "cut to."

If you watch Woody's early films—*Take the Money and Run, Sleeper*—sure they're funny. *He's* funny. But look at the shot composition. Notice the camera work and editing. Lots of cuts. Lots of zooms. Then watch *Interiors, Stardust Memories, Manhattan, Zelig, The Purple Rose of Cairo,* or virtually anything else shot by Gordon Willis. Then watch them again. Gordy moves the camera judiciously. He often composes shots in a tableau or proscenium style, which means that a scene is choreographed within static frame lines and has little or no coverage. Look at the shot composition in one of Gordy's films. Often a scene plays before a stationary camera, the actors walking in and out of frame, the dialogue spoken by an actor offscreen, and the background soft at times due to the chosen focal length, changing as the audience's attention moves within the scene. Then, perhaps in the middle of the scene, the stationary camera begins to move, to track with the actors as the scene is played out off-camera or in another room but still within the same uncut piece of film. It has all the great qualities of still photography: framing, composition, lighting. In fact, scenes shot in this style give the illusion that one is watching a still photo with movement within the frame.

Gordon Willis is a self-defined minimalist. He is so technically meticulous that he used antique camera lenses and duplicated newsreel lighting in *Zelig*. His contribution to the films he shoots defines the best of what a great DP can aspire to be. He integrates the photographic style with the story so well that the two are inseparable. In Gordy's hands, and through his eye, the cinematography becomes a character in the film. One who gives a brilliant, captivating, and well-crafted performance without being self-conscious, distracting, or self-indulgent.

Take virtually any shot in any of his films and you will understand why a great cinematographer is worth his weight in gold; it's because a great cinematographer is a true artist. The DP, along with the director, composes the film. In *A Midsummer Night's Sex Comedy,* there is a scene where Ariel (Mia Farrow) is on the couch after dinner and Maxwell (Tony Roberts) is speaking to her through the window behind where she is sitting as he literally swings on a hammock in and out of frame. Simply brilliant shot design. Part Woody. Part Gordy. Twenty-four-carat gold.

My favorite shot in *Stardust Memories*? The scene where we first see Sandy Bates in his apartment. After a few initial cuts, we pan through the apartment as the actors walk in and out of frame. At one point the camera takes a shortcut, tracking through a different room from the one the actors are in. There is a subtle push in on Sandy as we continue to pan, ending with the camera holding on a blank wall. The screen is completely empty. It is stark, innovative, unexpected, visually arresting. That's not cinematography; that's CINEMATOGRAPHY. The collaborative dance and interwoven threads of director and cinematographer seamlessly stitched and perfectly rendered.

Unlike Gordon Willis, Carlo Di Palma, another gifted cinematographer, who collaborated with Woody Allen on twelve films, including *Radio Days* and *Bullets Over Broadway,* moved the camera with greater freedom. *Husbands and Wives* is an extreme example of this. It is handheld, very stylized and intimate, very different from the look of the films Gordy shot. It represents a conscious decision by Woody in both designing the look of the film and in his choice of Carlo to shoot it. Watch *Crimes and Misdemeanors* or *Another Woman.* If Gordon is about the room, then Sven Nykvist was about the face. Look at the close-ups and skin tones; the well-lit emotion he captures in the face. None of this just happens by accident.

Selecting a DP is the first step toward defining the photographic style of a film. When you are working with a truly great cinematographer, like Gordon Willis, not a day goes by when you don't recognize the depth of his talent. At any given moment, it may be for either his artistic vision or his technical expertise.

The litmus test for great cinematography? Turn the volume on your television set off and start flipping through the movie channels. Don't worry about when a film started or who is in it. Forget the guide with the list of movie titles, and don't

47

stop at anything you have seen before. Strip the film down to its photographic bones by removing a few layers. The film viewed without the complement of plot, music, or dialogue leaves you with just framing, lighting, and shot design and will allow you to focus solely on the cinematography. Void of expectation, keep channel surfing until you catch a near-perfect shot. Maybe it will be the lighting that stops you in your tracks, or perhaps the way the camera moves, or the near-perfect, eye-catching, visually riveting nature of the framing. The film may be half over, you may have no idea what it is about, but you are hooked, entranced by what is on the screen. Continue to stay with the film, leaving the sound off. Chances are, that shot, the one that caused you to pause in the first place, wasn't an accident. It was talent. And chances are, there will be another great shot, and then another. When you are completely mesmerized by the cinematography, go to the guide and check out the title. Then find out who shot it. Every time I do this, I find gold. Try it and see if you don't stumble upon someone great: Giuseppe Rotunno, Vittorio Storaro, Michael Ballhaus, Dariusz Wolski, John Seale, Stephen Goldblatt, Dion Beebe . . .

A great cinematographer makes a rock-solid, indisputable contribution to both the art and the craft of a film. And you will appreciate his worth because you will be face-to-face with his technical skill every moment of the shooting day and again when the film hits the theaters and his artistic prowess is up on the screen. The spot gold price as of this writing? Seven hundred eighty-seven dollars an ounce, which would make a 165-pound cinematographer worth in the ballpark of $2 million. Your average feature film will make that at the box office in a few hours on opening weekend, and the great cinematographers contribution to the art? Immeasurable. A great cinematographer is truly worth his weight in gold.

12

SEAL THE DEAL WITH A GREAT OPERATOR.

IMAGINE hiring a wedding photographer who is not very good. He lops off the top of the bride's head, has trouble keeping the camera steady at times, and consistently misses what could be great shots because he can't seem to get them in focus or perfectly framed. No matter how well planned and executed the wedding is, no matter how beautiful the bride and the setting, ultimately it is the photographer who records it on film. Sure, he can ask the bride and groom to stage that first kiss again because he didn't quite get it, or ask the flower girl to make that adorable expression just one more time. He can continually restage and reshoot, but it will drag down the day, the shots will lose freshness and originality, and the photographs you end up with will be a testament to his lack of skill.

Now translate this to film photography. You have a great DP and director designing the shots. The blocking and the lighting are perfect. You have an experienced crew, all of whom have worked tirelessly to craft every element of every scene in the film. From the talented designers, expert makeup and hair people, the top property and wardrobe personnel to the stellar cast capable of world-class performances. Yet, if the camera operator isn't top-notch, if he keeps blowing the takes because he missed his marks or overpanned, you will lose time, you will lose momentum, and you will lose quality.

The Big Picture

Let's head back to our six-year-old flower girl. If she is playing a role in your movie instead of your wedding, she will be asked to replicate those adorable facial expressions as well as her lines until all of the coverage for each scene is shot. Under normal circumstances, and depending on the way a scene is covered, that may be anywhere from two to twenty times. Not easy for a lot of adults, let alone most six-year-olds. If she nails it and everything else in the shot is perfect but the operator didn't frame properly, you will have to do it again, which means time and money, the possibility of stale performances, or the director has to settle for a take he isn't thrilled with. And so begins the slow downhill slide set in motion by a mediocre camera operator.

Now back to my wedding photographer for a minute. By contrast, he has a far simpler task than the camera operator on a feature film. Comparatively speaking, he has to point and click. While a still shot has to be in focus and has to be composed and framed, a motion-picture shot is a series of rapid still photographs taken at the rate of twenty-four per second, and the focus and framing is far more complex. Throw in a moving camera, moving actors, changing depths of field, complicated lighting and staging, and you can begin to appreciate the technical skills required for an A-list operator.

Obviously, the cameras that we use to shoot feature films are nothing like the wedding photographer's camera or even the video camera you may have at home. A motion-picture camera usually requires three or four highly trained technicians to run and, depending on the shot, may be mounted on a dolly gliding on tracks, or on a crane arm so it can be lifted off of the ground or out over water. It may be handheld, resting on the shoulder of the operator, rigged in the back of a truck, or mounted in a helicopter. There are splash boxes and underwater housings. If it is stationary, it may be set on legs (a tripod) or a sandbag or on top of a ladder. To further complicate the process of film photography, the motion-picture camera is attached to a head, which is what the operator uses to tilt, pan, or swivel. So, imagine now that the camera is moving on dolly tracks, pushed into position by a grip who is following tape marks on the floor. At the same time, the operator pans or tilts the head and the first assistant cameraman pulls focus while the scene is being performed. Remember that not only is the camera moving but the actors and background are moving as well. Lines are being delivered and sound is being recorded as the action of the scene is being performed. The entire staged scene is unfolding before the camera, and it is the operator who is responsible for capturing it on film.

To illustrate the mechanics of what a camera operator actually does, and why it is so difficult to do well, consider that, just like our wedding photographer, the camera operator must "get the shot," which means handle the camera moves accurately and smoothly. And he must do it consistently well, whether Al Pacino is in front of the camera, or a stuntman doing a full-body burn, or an animal or a child is giving the performance of his life. Also consider that an actor has only so many takes in him. A dramatic or emotional scene, a difficult stunt, a choreographed dance sequence, a stylized shot with complicated blocking, are all extremely difficult to pull off. And sometimes the scene is shot under circumstances that require speed. For example, at sunset, when you have time for only one or two takes before losing the light. As a director, you don't want to have a great performance blown because the operator simply couldn't make the shot. You don't want the camera operator asking for another rehearsal because the shot is too difficult for him to get, and you don't want a complicated shot ruined with jerking camera movements or because the operator missed his marks and overpanned as an actor stood up from a chair.

That channel-surfing game I play to discover great cinematographers? I like to play it when looking for great operators, too. Again, turn off the sound on your television. Don't note when the movie started or who is in it, or even if the plot holds together. Forget the lighting and shot design, because that's the work of the director and DP. Just observe the camera work. Whenever I do this, whenever I find the rock-steady pans, the perfect framing, the smooth, unflinching, exacting camera moves I learned to expect when working with great operators, I know it will be a name I recognize. Maybe it's the work of Dick Mingalone, who handled those complicated shots designed by Gordon Willis and Woody Allen with ease—those long tracking shots and moving masters—with no monitor to confirm that he got the shot, just his skill and eye and steady hand behind the camera. I know it's very likely that when a film is over and I read the end credits, if the operating was flawless, it will be one of the greats: Dick Mingalone, Tommy Priestley Jr., Bruce MacCallum, Ray De La Motte. . . . Those unsung heroes of cinematography who consistently get the shot. The operators. Great cinematographers may be worth their weight in gold, but always seal the deal with a great operator.

13

SHOOT ON A LOW FLOOR.

WOODY Allen shoots most of his films in New York City. You could say that he has had a cinematic love affair with its people and streets, filming her bridges, her boroughs, her storefronts and parks, from Madison Square Garden to the Carnegie Deli, from Tavern on the Green to a flophouse on the Lower East Side. Exposing not only her character but her characters. Filming both her architecture and her personality while showcasing his personal haunts, from John's Pizza and Elaine's to Mia Farrow's apartment, Woody has immortalized New York.

In so doing, he has captured the city in both black and white and in Technicolor, in its period detail and its contemporary splendor, the fantastic and the ordinary. He's dressed her to the nines and photographed her stark naked, in stolen shots with a hidden camera as he walked down her teeming streets. Whether shooting the Waldorf-Astoria or the Bowery, as a filmmaker, Woody Allen *owns* Manhattan.

But New York is a vertical city and Woody hates to ride in elevators. So we would take to the stairs. Literally. An idiosyncrasy that has kept us, as filmmakers, by and large, pretty close to the ground floor. Sure, we've shot the occasional penthouse. That apartment with a view. That perfect set on the tenth floor. On those days when the crew took to the elevators, Woody and

I would take to the stairs. It's not so bad, I'd say to myself. It's good exercise . . .

But there is reason beyond claustrophobia and cardiovascular stress to pick our locations close to the ground. If we go up, we may gain a view and lose street noise, but we take on a whole slew of logistical problems. Every single piece of equipment has to be transported into and out of any location. I'm talking tons. From the cameras and set dressing to lights, grip equipment, cast, and crew. This takes time and costs money. If a location is on a high floor, the load-in and load-out alone will take at least three hours out of the shooting day. And this is assuming we have prerigged the day before, roughing in lights and doing cable runs. On top of this, try sending a sixty-person crew and thirty extras to lunch at the same time with only one small elevator available to you.

If we're up high and there's only one elevator, it'll cost an extra ten grand in overtime for the crew, and every time we need an actor or something from the trucks, it'll take ten minutes. It becomes an expensive commute. Indeed, if we do a dozen setups over the course of a shooting day, the actors will spend an hour or more just going back and forth from their motor homes out on the street to the set on that upper floor.

Consider that even to shoot an interior, some of the lights have to be mounted *outside* the windows. Try that on the twenty-second floor. Your only option is a balcony, if there is one, because even a Condor, or bucket truck positioned on the street adjacent to the building, is limited to about three stories. In addition, consider that thousands of pounds of electrical cable have to run from a generator truck on the street up to the apartment where we will shoot. Harder to do the higher up we go.

So the specter of compromise rears its head. Ideally, as filmmakers, an apartment on the second floor is what we're looking for. It's accessible, easy to light, cost-effective. It's high enough to avoid the worst of the street noise, and if we really need a view out of a window, we can always shoot that separately with a splinter crew in an upper-floor apartment with the same floor plan and matching window dressing.

Scouting locations with a new director always takes me back to those days trudging up the stairs with Woody as I think, Avoid the city's canopy, stay low, light from the sidewalk, save on overtime and extra equipment. Develop a little claustrophobia and bypass the overcrowded elevator. Shoot on a low floor.

SHOOT IN FLAT LIGHT.

14

I know these two things. First, that there are approximately two hundred sunny days in New York City each year, and, second, that it's a good bet Woody Allen won't shoot exteriors on any one of them. With the exception of a few films like *A Midsummer Night's Sex Comedy,* where sunlight is important to the story line, if the sun is out, Woody will be on a "cover set," filming an interior. Watch a few of his films and try to find a bright sunny day or a long shadow. It's hard to do.

From a strictly artistic standpoint, flat light is beautiful because it provides a soft, even palette. In addition, it makes economic sense. Flat light is actually *cheaper* to shoot in than bright sunshine. Which means that shooting in flat light, because it's cost-effective and aesthetically desirable, serves both the art and the budget. While this sounds too good to be true, it isn't. Here's why.

Photography is, of course, light-dependant, and cinematography is, in its simplest form, a series of moving pictures. Which means we either offer the director and cinematographer a uniformly lit "canvas"—a day with flat light—or we spend time and money trying to control the sunlight. *And on a clear day, it is changing constantly.*

Shooting outside on a sunny day necessitates adding light, removing light, setting silks, avoiding shadows, and fighting with the sun as it crosses the sky. We must match every shot so it will cut seamlessly together in a sequence. The light has to match in a scene even if each shot was taken under radically different conditions. Remember, the sun moves across the sky in *real time* and we shoot in *movie time.* In other words, during a normal twelve-hour shooting day, while the sun has risen and set, we actually film only two to three minutes of "master time." Which means that any two shots we cut together, that you see in the finished film just a fraction of a second apart on screen, may actually have been shot hours or days or, in many cases, even weeks apart under different natural-light conditions.

The truth is, that with all of our money and virtually un-limited resources, we can't stop the sun from moving across the sky. As the great cinematographer Gordon Willis would often say with profound simplicity as he looked through the lens, "The Earth is rotating." While we can't stop it, as film-makers we still have to deal with it, which is expensive and time-consuming.

Or we can simply shoot on a flat day, which means under total cloud cover. Then we can move like lightning. There are no shadows. We can shoot north, south, east, or west at our prerogative. All the shots will cut together and match, thanks to the balance and uniformity of those slate gray skies. This style of filming requires less equipment and manpower and gives us the flexibility to really move the camera. Fast. In short, we can shoot in any direction, at any time, without panning into a "hot" building or avenue. Without bringing in cranes to hang diffusion. Without looking at our watches and compro-mising shots. It is smarter, cheaper, faster, and the end product is more beautiful. By shooting in flat light, we have, in a fash-ion, found a way to stop the Earth from rotating. Or at least, to erase any visual evidence of it.

When shooting the film *Just Cause* with Sean Connery in

the blazing Florida sun, we had to use a crane to suspend a forty-foot-by-forty-foot silk above the actors' heads, effectively removing the bright sun from the sky. It took us twelve hours to do eight camera setups as we continually battled the sun. Yet with Woody on *Hannah and Her Sisters,* under the perfect conditions of high cloud cover, we were able to do more than a dozen setups in an eight-hour day as we filmed Michael Caine pursuing Barbara Hershey through the streets of SoHo. We shot more material, with less equipment and manpower. We avoided meal penalties, overtime, and turnaround problems. We made the days work with less wear and tear on the actors, the crew, and the film's budget.

My favorite weather report? High cloud cover, with only a slight chance of rain. My credo: Don't wrestle with the sun; just stop the Earth from spinning. Shoot in flat light.

15

... UNLESS THE SUN PLAYS
A ROLE IN THE FILM.

STEP outside of your house or apartment at 7:00 A.M. on a sunny day and look at the light. Then do so again at noon and at four o'clock. Pretty basic, you think. The sun rises in the east, sets in the west, and sits directly overhead at noon. The shadows fall from east to west in the morning and reverse to fall west to east in the afternoon. But before you decide that a sunny day is a sunny day is a sunny day, take a walk around the block. Then do it two weeks later or in a different season or city. Check out another street. Notice anything different?

One block may be sunny; the next is draped in shadow. The north side of one street may be in constant shade, the south side the polar opposite—a blinding landscape of blazing sun. Take a moment to observe the impact that tall buildings have on light and shadow. Most cities like New York have entire blocks that are perpetual dark canyons, even on the sunniest of days. Note that the sun hangs lower in the sky in winter. Four o'clock in May looks different, radically different, than four o'clock in October or January. Sure, you think you know this already, but a filmmaker has to have a very exacting relationship with light.

Take a close look at a single month—say, November. It will be dark at exactly 4:29 P.M. in New York on November 30 (2009), but, by comparison, not until 8:31 P.M. on the first of July. Over the course of the month, we lose one hour and twenty-three minutes of light at the end of the day, while picking up twenty-seven minutes of light in the morning. And that's without calculating daylight saving time. Bear in mind also that to a filmmaker this battle with the sun is more than an issue of available daylight hours. As the shooting day unfolds and the sun is moving across the sky, you are also moving the camera and trying to match shots. It is maddening, but there is no negotiating. If you are shooting an exterior in bright daylight, you had better be well versed in the habits of the sun.

As the previous chapter explains, the simple solution when shooting exteriors is to shoot in flat light. While that won't change what time the sun sets or rises, it will at least eliminate issues of shade and shadow, hot spots and glare, fundamentally leveling the playing field and transplanting all locations to the shady side of the street. But what if sunlight is important to the film? What if, for artistic reasons, or because of certain story points, the director must shoot on bright, sunny days?

Woody Allen's film *A Midsummer Night's Sex Comedy* is a celebration of summer. The sun is critical to the theme of the movie and it, effectively, became part of the set dressing if not an actual character in the film. Since we couldn't shoot on flat days, Woody and Gordon Willis had to design the shots around the sun. Further complicating the solar equation, the story takes place over a single weekend, though we would need over four months to shoot it. Three days of "movie time" translated to four months of variations in weather and light. Under these circumstances, continuity of light takes on a whole new perspective.

Take, for example, a single scene we called "Fun at the Brook." It was scene twenty-three in the script and was 2⅛ pages in length. This scene was staged as six people (three couples) walked back from a picnic to Maxwell's country home. Standard coverage on a scene like this in many films would often entail an establishing shot, a master of the entire scene, and medium shots on each actor, then close-ups. By most standards, this would represent one or more days of work. Matching light for a single scene shot over such a long time period would be very time-consuming. But to Gordon and Woody, it represented only several hours of work, a block of time much closer to the real time and light patterns of the picnic we were shooting. And because the shot was designed as a moving master, the issue of matching light fell away from the equation.

Rather than singles, two shots, and standard coverage, Woody and Gordon devised a stylish method of covering the scene in one elegant, elaborate setup done with a long dolly shot. Commencing with a stationary camera, the six actors approached, in three rows of two. As they neared, the camera tracked with them. The dolly adjusted its speed to the pace of the actors, thereby allowing the actors to go from a wide six-shot into a tighter medium one, and then to a four-shot, three-shot, and ultimately a two-shot. The camera slid along the rails until, at a certain point, it stopped and panned with the actors, who walked away in a six-shot, completing their dialogue while the camera held a final wide graphic.

In essence, what Woody and Gordy shot was a wide establishing shot, a medium shot, two six-shots, a tracking shot for coverage, and a final wide graphic. What would have been ten setups for another DP and director was accomplished in one. The design of the shot, coupled with the brevity of time needed to shoot it (hours rather than days), allowed the entire sequence to be filmed in perfect natural light that matched. We weren't fighting and racing with the sun; we were basking in it. Had we shot standard coverage for this scene over a day or two, we would have had to utilize lots of diffusion and additional lights to compensate for the sun as it moved across the sky and we moved the camera.

The Big Picture

Woody and Gordon had to find another creative solution to pin down the sun in order to film the outdoor dinner scene, which ran about three minutes in length. To cover it, we grabbed the shots, a few setups per day, in the late afternoon, over the course of two weeks. In order to get all of the work in the matching early-evening light, each day at the same time we stopped our other work and returned to the dinner scene. Just think about the logistics of restaging this scene every day. Wardrobe, hair and makeup, continuity of set dressing and performance. The same scene repeated each afternoon until all of the coverage had been shot in the perfect replica of the previous day's light. Scheduled this way solely to accommodate and to match the light.

Another option to avoid expensive and complicated exterior lighting is to lay out the shots for a scene in such a way that the segments that will be cut together will be shot in matching or complementary light conditions, regardless of the time of day, so that a light change will not be evident.

Which is exactly what Gordon Willis did for the softball scene in Jim Toback's *The Pick-up Artist*. Gordy laid out the shots with the precision of a mathematician. In the scene, Jack Jericho (Robert Downey, Jr.) brings his class of ten-year-olds to Central Park to play softball. Even though we shot twelve setups in eight hours, the continuity of light is seamless. With the sun constantly moving across the sky, this was accomplished by the concise and calculated manner in which Gordon laid out each shot, then determined the order in which they should be filmed, based on the sun's path over the course of the day. His time was spent walking around the diamond during the blocking rehearsal as he considered backlight, shadows, and the equipment needs in consort with the action required in each sequence. We had to photograph the pitcher as well as the batter, the infielders, outfielders, runners, and fans, and the light had to be perfect even when many hours separated shots that would be a split second apart on-screen. To an outsider, the shooting order that evolved out of our shot list may have seemed haphazard—say shots number eight, four, and one, then three, seven, and nine. Yet it was anything but. Instead, it was the antithesis of random. It was exacting. The scene works beautifully because the light is balanced and the colors are rich, even though the pitcher threw the ball at 8:00 A.M. and the batter swung at 3:30.

When planning scenes to be shot exterior and in the sun, we have to consider the schedule of the sun, just like we do with any actor. A cast member may have to be through on set by six o'clock because she is appearing in a play on Broadway, and the sun may have to be wrapped by 4:37 because it is appearing in the southern hemisphere. The movie will have to be scheduled around the timetables of both of them. We must also take into account that, unlike most actors, even when it is on the set, the sun doesn't stand still. Ever. Nor will it appear on certain sides of the street or volunteer to go where you want it to. And it never, ever does night work.

When you are able to, shoot in flat light. But if you have no choice, due to budget or schedule restrictions, or if the sun plays a role in the film, meet it head-on. Since the sun won't negotiate, remember that you have no choice but to navigate around it. You can design a single master shot and shoot your scene in a few hours. Or do the math and lay out your shots so they will cut together in perfect sync with the light. Or make a date with the sun. Say four o'clock every day for the entire week. Then dissect the scene and shoot it, one camera setup at a time, in the natural matching light. Without the blanket of those high clouds or the artificial diffusion of silks and shade, you're going to need a plan if the sun plays a role in the film.

16

THE COLOR PALETTE IS CRITICAL.

THINK that's a raspberry pink dress? The wardrobe people may think so . . . and to your eye it certainly *looks* pink. Well, think again. That dress may, in fact, not be raspberry pink, or even close to the shade of pink your eye sees when it debuts on-screen.

When making a movie, you have to consider that the color of everything that will appear on-screen will depend not on how it is seen by the human eye, but on how it is seen by the camera lens and captured on film. Not only the wardrobe and that raspberry pink dress, but everything from set dressing and the color of the lawn to paint on the walls, hair color, makeup, and props.

For starters, color is affected by light, and light is dependant on many variables. Will that dress be in a scene that will be shot at an interior location or an exterior? Will it be day or night? How will the scene be lit? What t-stop will the DP be shooting at, and which lens will he be using? What will be the impact of colored gels on the lights, or CTO on the windows, or filters in the camera? What film stock and ASA rating will be used? Then you have to factor in how the film will be processed at the lab. How will the film be timed and printed? Every one of these elements, individually and collectively, will affect color.

And before you settle on that dress you think might possibly be raspberry pink, consider what color the walls will be painted on the set where the dress will be worn. What color are the chairs in the room where the actress wearing that dress will be seated? Have you ever picked which clothes you will wear based on the color of the chair you will be sitting in, or what the other guests in the room might be wearing? Probably not. But if you are directing a movie, you have to consider the color of everything and how it will play against all the other colors in each scene. Take note that the costume designer probably hasn't even seen most of the sets. Therefore he won't know if his wardrobe selection will clash with the set decoration or potentially blend in too much. While you usually don't want colors to jump out on screen, you also can't have an actress in a green dress on a green couch, either, or you may end up with a "talking head" in a sea of green.

Next, you have to consider the palette of contiguous scenes. Remember, a movie is not shot in sequence, so today's scene with that raspberry pink dress and green couch may cut to a scene with a canary yellow blouse that you shoot a month later and that could be chromatically loud and visually jarring. Multiply this by the sixty or seventy different actors and as many sets in a film and it quickly becomes clear that all of this will take some meticulous planning. But don't forget that your eyes may deceive you. Remember, you're not even sure what shade of pink that dress is anymore. Doing night shots in an automobile? Pick its color carefully. Silver and gray are good choices. Black or white less so (white is too hot and black too difficult to read). And the seats should be a light color to provide separation from the actors sitting in them. Whether wardrobe, set decoration, or props, the variables multiply exponentially.

My advice? Forget the possibly pink dress. Stick with a warm, soft palette. To the degree that you can, take harsh color out of the equation. Do what Woody does and stay muted and warm. Create a color scheme that is harmonious, not chaotic.

The Big Picture

Think beige and brown, burgundy, soft green, rust. Choose colors that will blend and complement each other so that nothing will clash or pop out, but still think about contrast and separation. If you do, your scenes will cut together and blend perfectly as far as color goes. Design the entire movie in one color palette and then, if you want, use color intentionally and selectively as a dramatic and artistic element. Think about the red coat on the little girl in Steven Spielberg's *Schindler's List,* or Woody's selective use of color in *The Purple Rose of Cairo,* or the brilliant and calculated use of color in films like *The Wizard of Oz, Pleasantville, The Sixth Sense,* or *Le Ballon Rouge.* And if you do go bold, make sure it is by design, not random chance or poor planning. Make a statement with color. Think John Waters and *Hairspray* or Mel Stuart and *Willy Wonka and the Chocolate Factory.*

Before you settle on a palette, consider removing color altogether by shooting in black and white. Take a look at *Manhattan* and *Broadway Danny Rose* and see how gradations of black, white, and gray can be the very best choice of all. But don't fall victim to thinking that shooting in black and white is a simple way out of the color equation, either, since every color has a black-and-white value, and that requires calculated planning, too. That raspberry pink dress won't be black or white; it will be somewhere in between on the gray scale. Where? You'll have to do camera tests to find out.

The most important thing to remember is not to make the mistake of thinking that anything is accidental or will "just work." In a good film, everything is painstakingly planned and executed. Don't trust your eyes; assume you're color-blind. Calculate. Plan. Test film emulsions and makeup, costumes and filters. Control is the name of the game. Coordinate wardrobe and set design. Use color intentionally and deliberately. Don't let it be an innocent bystander or a tragic victim. The color palette is critical.

MOVE INTO YOUR CAR.

17

ON an average feature film, we normally shoot a minimum of twelve-hour days. We often work outside in the elements, at odd hours and radically different locations. A frozen pond one day, a meatpacking plant the next, perhaps followed by a string of nights on a rooftop in the Bronx, or a day with an elephant at Jones Beach. Each location is uniquely challenging, offering varying climates and circumstances.

My first film with Woody? *Stardust Memories* in 1979. One of the first days of shooting? A scene in which three eighty-foot-high hot-air balloons were launched from a field on Long Island out in the parching sun. Since I took the crew bus back then, traveling from Manhattan to each new day's location, I was forced to pack everything I might need into a shoulder bag. A copy of the script, the actors' sides (script pages), call sheets, some pencils, a bunch of quarters for the pay phones, maybe some sunscreen. But I learned quickly that being prepared means being comfortable. Standing out in the elements for so many hours always leaves you wishing you had remembered just one more thing. So I got a bigger bag.

Now I pack the trunk of my car. Spiked shoes for walking across ice? Got them. Hip boots for standing in water? Ditto. Goose-down jacket, ski pants, hand warmers, rain gear, multiple changes of clothes, wet suit? Of course. Maps, power bars, corkscrew, face mask, paint thinner, a copy of last year's taxes? All a given.

Who would think, as they prepared to leave for work in the morning, that later that day they might be dive-bombed by a pelican or peed on by an actor? (Okay, the actor was a one-year-old, but still it meant a change of pants.)

The pelican encounter took place on a dock in Sarasota, Florida, while shooting *Great Expectations.* In the scene we were filming, Robert De Niro, who was playing the convict, Lustig, had to leap out of Finn's boat and swim to a marker buoy to hide from an approaching Coast Guard cutter. The director, Alfonso Cuarón, wanted to shoot the scene with seagulls circling in the backdrop of the sky, so the props started chumming to attract them. We were fighting the light, the gulls, the dynamics of boats, actors, and stuntmen in the water, and, as always, the clock. As I stood on the dock preparing the shot, a large dark shadow passed overhead. I looked up, saw the underbelly not of a cloud or a small aircraft, but of a giant bird, and then—bam! It suddenly felt like I had been hit in the back with a softball. A pelican had nailed me. Not exactly something you can plan for. My shirt hit the nearest trash bin and, without breaking stride, I dispatched a production assistant to my car to retrieve another one.

The diaperless baby was for a sequence in Taylor Hackford's film *The Devil's Advocate,* where Mary Ann, played by Charlize Theron, has a dream about a naked baby playing with a pile of entrails. During filming, I was just off-camera, setting the baby up for each shot and handling her in between takes. About twenty minutes into the sequence, while she sat on my lap, I felt a warm sensation spreading across my thigh. Again back to my car. Hand wipes, clean socks, dry jeans, a splash of cologne, and I was good to go. So I've learned to be prepared. But not just for pelicans and babies.

MOVE INTO YOUR CAR.

My car is not only my closet; it's my home office and my workside cabana. In it, I do paperwork, conduct interviews, catch my breath, touch base with home. My car is my haven from the chaos of the set as well as my favorite restaurant. I've driven down Madison Avenue more than once with a second AD cooking hamburgers on a portable grill. I kid you not.

On difficult days, when we break for lunch, I often retreat to the peace and solitude of that front seat, pop open the glove compartment, where I keep a collection of take-out menus from neighborhood restaurants from all over the city, and order in. Nobody from the crew, with their litany of questions, will dare bother me here. Part phone booth and part deli counter, part desk chair and part isolation chamber, my car has become a rarified, almost holy place. Oh, and when you phone in an order to a restaurant and tell them your address is the dark blue Jeep parked on the corner of Broadway and Ninety-sixth Street, nobody misses a beat. After all, it's New York, and you can get just about anything delivered. Even to your car.

My advice? Be prepared. When shooting a movie, all bets are off. Assume the worst. Don't just pack the normal stuff; go for the exotic. On some films, a Hungarian dictionary may be more valuable than antibacterial wipes. But you never know, so bring them both. Even though your call sheet lists each and every location, pack like you have no idea where you are going or when you might ever get to come back. Plan ahead. Move into your car.

18

THE STRIP BOARD IS THE ROSETTA STONE OF FILMMAKING.

WHEN Napoléon's troops unearthed the Rosetta stone, it provided the key for deciphering all of the ancient Egyptian writing that had baffled historians for thousands of years. The same passage written in three languages providing an old school decoder ring for Egyptian hieroglyphics. A movie strip board, with its color-coded pictorial and numeric symbols, does the same thing for a film shoot.

While the text is not actually carved in stone, and a strip board is constructed of a slab of compressed cardboard, not granite or basalt, the board is, without question, a multilingual stela that serves as the key to understanding the production. It is assembled from the thousands of individual factoids that are recorded during the breakdown of the script. The key elements of each scene are transcribed first to a breakdown sheet and then to a cardboard strip. This process distills the story down to its nuts and bolts, the structural components left void of any narrative or plot. The scenes are numbered, the strips color-coded: yellow for exterior day, white for interior, blue for exterior night. A black strip denotes the end of each shooting day, a red strip the end of a week. Each actor in a scene is numerically coded, along with locations, picture cars, cranes, stunts, special effects, number of extras . . . every detail of the scene extrapolated from the script and rerecorded onto a strip.

If the script has a hundred scenes, the board will have a hundred strips. These thin pieces of cardboard are then assembled into a frame, or board, that serves as a visual blueprint for the film. Each strip, or scene, is placed in the board in the order that it will be shot, not the sequential order of the script, thus rendering the board both a visual and tactile map of the production as well as the step-by-step directions for getting from the first scene, and the first day, to the last.

In preproduction, the board sets the framework, providing a sort of loose outline or rough draft of the shoot. Then, as we wend our way closer to the first day of shooting, it becomes more rigid, taking on the status of a royal decree. Need to know where we are shooting on day twenty-three or how many extras we need in week four? Is the leading man needed on February 24? When are we scheduled to shoot nights? Can we move the fight scene closer to the end of the film? What happens if it snows in week one? Every answer is right there on the board.

If it rains and we move to a cover set, or we lose a location and our schedule is altered, the strips are instantly adjusted to reflect this new development. Everything we need to know about that shift and its ripple effect will become visually evident on the board. Everything from changes in actor spreads (availability) to the number of extras or motor homes we may need on any given day is a mere glance away. The board provides definitive answers in a very concrete and readily accessible form.

While the strip board will provide a physical and visual blueprint of the movie, I also know that the real work comes not in the bare bones of the board, not in the who, what, where, but in the how. The translation of those hieroglyphics into the physical, practical, and financial realities of film production.

For example, take the opening scene of *Evening,* directed

by the acclaimed Hungarian cinematographer and director Lajos Koltai (*Fateless*), which was just barely over a page in length and called for flying insects, fog and wind special effects, a prerecorded song to be played back over speakers while we shot, and a small sailboat in the ocean with its sail up yet stationary (held in place by anchors and scuba divers). All of this information was coded and transferred onto a single yellow (for exterior day) cardboard strip.

With the board open in front of me, I would instantly know by looking at the strip for this scene that it calls for a sailboat (indicated by a square), playback of a prerecorded song (PB), and special effects (FX). The notation of "FX" on the strip referencing not only fog and wind special effects but the fact that the screen was to fill with flying insects. (For some special effects, in this case insects fluttering on screen, it is just impractical to shoot live and it is more efficient to create it with computers than to try to get real insects to actually do what we want on camera so these were computer generated.) This strip also carried the notation of the numerical code for Patrick Wilson, and that of "MU," indicating the need for special makeup, which was required for the aging of Patrick, who was playing the role of both the young and the older Harris Arden in the film. I would also know by glancing at the strip that if we wanted to shoot at daybreak, Patrick would need a 3:00 A.M. call so he could get through the three to four hours of special makeup and hair that were needed to age him those forty years. The notation of the "C" on the strip indicated that we were shooting the scene with a crane, which carried its own set of encumbrances, including the need to build a road in the sand on the beach where we would be shooting and get permits from the city. The words in the script—"a woman standing on a rock in the middle of the water"—translated to the strip as "ocean, rocks." But placing a seventy-plus-year-old actress, Eileen Atkins (and later Vanessa Redgrave), on a rock in the ocean in an evening dress takes some serious thought. The scene, and strip, also called for putting Ann Grant (Claire Danes) along with Harris out in a sailboat in the ocean. (Eventually, when we shot, we built a ramp so that Eileen could safely walk out onto the rocks, and we physically carried Claire Danes through the shallow water and put her into the boat so her costume would not get wet.) I also knew just from looking at the strip that the proximity to the water would mean we would need duplicate costumes in case one of the actors got wet. All of this information instantly gleaned from a few notations on a cardboard strip.

As we get closer to actual production, the board becomes the basis for a document called the "shooting schedule," and eventually all of the information from the board is transcribed from the shooting schedule onto the call sheet, which outlines the following days' work and is handed out to everyone on the crew before the end of each shooting day. The board, with its highly distilled and coded information, essentially takes us from the script to the street. From the written word and conceptual plan to the physical production of a film.

But technology is a soft sell in the film business, and, unfortunately, the strip board as I know it is rapidly becoming somewhat of an ancient artifact. Something worthy of a film-production museum as computer programs now create a facsimile, a kind of "cyber board." The strips and schedule now often computer-generated, not hand-tooled. So when I show up on a film with a traditional strip board, I feel a bit like an Egyptian in robes carting an antiquated slab of basalt. Young production people stand back, almost in awe, as I flip open the board and show them my hieroglyphic pencil scrawling and then pick up strips and move scenes and days around as I demonstrate the enormous impact on schedule and budget that moving a few strips of cardboard can have.

The new computer-generated boards? Personally, I'll

take Sharpies and pressed cardboard over titanium and megabytes. For me at least, I learn the film at the other end of a sharp pencil and a cardboard strip. It is in the process of making the board, and scheduling the movie by moving those strips around, that I really get to know the project. The tough weeks, the rationale behind the schedule, the ins and outs of actors' spreads, all etched into my neural pathways as they are inked onto the cardboard strips.

With the board open on my desk during preproduction, or on the back of my car in the pouring rain late at night on day three of shooting, I can see all twelve weeks at a glance. On the computer, you get only one page at a time. And I can usually answer a question, or make and defend a decision, while the guy with the laptop is still waiting to boot up.

The ability to create an efficient and makeable shooting schedule is about the disciplined management of thousands of interdependent pieces of information. It takes years of accumulated experience to be able to do it well. I know about how many camera setups will be needed for a car chase, what rain does to actors' hair, how night shooting affects turnaround (sleep and get back on a day schedule), what is involved in moving locations, the impact of working with children. I know the union rules and the human factor and how they translate to time and money and page count. So when my cardboard strip says "rain FX," or "exterior night," I don't have to translate that into Greek, demotic Egyptian, or computer code but just from the hieroglyphs to a makeable shooting day.

19

WHAT SHOULD BE IN YOUR BACK POCKET WHEN YOU SHOW UP ON SET?

IF the strip board contains all of the information necessary to shoot an entire film, my back pocket contains all of the information needed to shoot for a single day. When I leave for work, stuffed into the back pocket of my jeans is the call sheet, which lists all of the scenes we will shoot that day, as well as every element necessary to do so: the actors, props, vehicles, any special FX, the crew names and contact information, what time and where we will be working, as well as an advance schedule for the next few days, and any and all other specific and pertinent data. Just the hard elements, the nuts and bolts that were first pulled from the script, transposed to breakdown sheets, transcribed onto the strip board, and printed on a shooting schedule during preproduction have now found their way onto the call sheet and into the hands and pockets of everyone on the crew.

Stapled to the call sheet are the sides, or script pages, for the current scenes we are shooting. Finally, and of equal importance, in my pocket on every single shooting day, are the sides for the scenes that will come immediately before and after the ones we are currently filming, a habit I picked up from working with Woody. Invaluable for the very simple reason that a director has to think not only about the look of each individual scene but the look of the whole film and how it will be cut together, as well.

The Big Picture

It is important to have the connecting scenes for both ends of any scene "in your back pocket" because you can't lay out the shots for the current day's work properly unless you know how the previous scenes will end and the following scenes will begin. Remember that even though directors see each previous day's work in dailies, and may edit as they go along, abutting scenes are often shot weeks or even months apart. A good director is always cognizant of the bookending scenes to remind him what he is cutting from or to. Scenes do not stand by themselves. They transition from one to the next.

For example, if the previous scene ends with a tight close-up of an actor's face, you may not want to open the next scene with another tight close-up. (Although, then again you might.) Maybe it's better to start this scene wide. It's that simple, but also that complex. And that following scene? Though you may not have shot it yet, or, indeed, may have finished it a month ago, either way, the scene you will shoot today will be cutting to it and you will want the image you end with to cut to the next scene in a seamless manner.

The transitions between scenes need to be smooth, with careful attention paid to shot selection, the flow of dialogue, and consistency in pacing. Some directors are so fastidious that they lay out the entire movie by storyboarding it before day one of shooting begins. Other directors work more in a "fly by the seat of the pants," day-to-day method. But nobody any good is doing it haphazardly or without some kind of planning. Woody may not plan the day's shots until he is on the set on any given day, but he absolutely considers the abutting scenes and how they were, or will be, shot. And it isn't just the design of the shot, the camera angle, or the frame size that have to be considered. What is the emotional tenor of the abutting scenes? How about the camera movement, lighting, or the last character in frame? What dramatic or comedic point is being made?

WHAT SHOULD BE IN YOUR BACK POCKET

The more planning, the more preediting that is done as you shoot, the more streamlined the editing process, and the better the film will be. It is enormously helpful to know what you will be cutting from and what you are cutting to. This guarantees that, at the very least, a well-thought-out transition between each scene will have been filmed. Having those few extra pages stuffed in your back pocket will go a long way toward ensuring this.

FACE THE REALITIES OF THE BUDGET. EVEN FIFTY MILLION WON'T SEEM LIKE ENOUGH.

20

IF you want to be a painter, a hundred bucks will get you a canvas and some oils. Turpentine and brushes are not very likely to break the bank. A writer needs even less—perhaps just some blank paper and a couple of sharp pencils. Musicians can get their fingers on some keys or strings without the backing of an investment bank. Most artists, in fact, can explore their field without the help of a private equity firm. But the average feature film costs about fifty million dollars to produce. That's roughly what it costs to buy a Picasso oil painting, a 737 from Boeing, or a 20 percent share of the Chrysler Building. Film is, hands down, the most expensive form of artistic expression. Which is why film, as an art form, is almost never completely free of commercial and financial restraints.

To examine why a feature film is so expensive to produce, we should begin with the actual canvas itself, the film stock, which runs over six hundred dollars for a magazine (a one-thousand-foot roll.) Each magazine contains ten minutes worth of 35-mm film, and a feature length movie requires about two hundred of them. Which means that the raw film stock alone costs about $125,000. While you will eventually have to allocate another $100,000 in lab fees, before you can develop the film you have to develop the project. Using Writers Guild of America minimums, you will have to allocate at least five or six figures to buy a script, followed by fees for a producer and a director, pay legal and financing costs, then set up an office, hire a casting agent and department heads. Unfortunately, unlike those for a painter or musician, these setup and development costs are only the front end of the equation.

When making a film, you have to budget for equipment and location rentals, construction and travel, and the cost of a full crew. Expenses that, collectively, will reach well into the millions. That's millions of dollars either spent or committed to be spent before the director applies a single brush stroke to the very expensive canvas of a feature film. You may have already spent millions, yet not a single foot of film has been shot.

During the shooting period, the project will run up costs resembling Third World debt, and the money starts burning up like jet fuel on the tarmac, which, by the way, cost about sixty thousand dollars when we shot a scene for Bill Murray and Howard Franklin's *Quick Change,* using an airplane on the runway of Newark Liberty International Airport. One scene, six hours, sixty thousand dollars for a jet and fuel, and we didn't even taxi or take off. Actually, we didn't move an inch. That's just what it cost to idle. And that was just to get the exterior airplane scene. To shoot the interior of the plane, we had to fly a crew down to Florida to a soundstage where MGM had a mockup of a jetliner that could readily accommodate the lights and camera equipment, the crew and the shots the directors wanted. Feature-film equipment just doesn't fit or move around very well on a real airplane. Or in a real car, for that matter. Shooting a scene inside a limousine? You might need to cut the roof out of one, as we did on *Nothing But the Truth,* to get the Steadicam shot the director, Rod Lurie, envisioned. Then leave room in the budget for a second car if you want to actually see it without the roof cut out. In filmmaking, things that appear simple and ordinary are often extraordinarily expensive to pull off.

The Big Picture

Motor homes, trucks, crew vans, and teamsters could run $600,000 to $1 million on a big studio picture. A big star or two? Well, the sky is the limit, but fifteen to twenty million a-piece, plus the milk and cookies for their favorite drivers and hairstylists. The perks for some stars can run over a million dollars.

Want to grab some shots for two days in Mexico? Add a minimum of $400,000 to $500,000 to the budget to hire a crew to prep and shoot. Special effects? Construction? Just depends on the parameters of the script and the director's vision for each scene. But hard costs like camera equipment? A typical package will run $25,000 a week. The grip and electric package will run another $20,000 per week for the shooting period. A twelve-week shoot translates to over $600,000 for lights and camera equipment even before anyone says "Action."

Wardrobe on an average picture, assuming you don't need anything special, is budgeted in the hundreds of thousands of dollars. Location rentals? Ballpark another $500,000, assuming you don't need anything special here, either. A scene on a subway train or at the Metropolitan Museum of Art will run $30,000 to $40,000 to buy that location just for a single day. Stunts are almost always very expensive. Have a car chase with a Mercedes? You might need half a dozen of them to dent up and twenty or thirty stuntmen to drive the other cars in the scene. A single car chase can take over a week to film and often costs over a million dollars.

Casting a child? You're paying a tutor, and the child is re-stricted to a six- to eight-hour workday. Want one hundred extras in the background for a party scene or while your prin-cipal actors walk down Fifth Avenue? Each extra will run you about two hundred dollars for a twelve-hour shooting day, in-cluding overtime and fringes. Which doesn't seem that bad until you consider that you may need three thousand of them over the course of an average fifty-day shoot, which translates to over half a million dollars just for the background extras. That's half a million dollars for the people crossing the street and standing at the bus stop. And I'm not talking about a big film like *Gandhi,* which may require thousands of extras for just a single day.

Creative decisions in film, on one level or another, are frequently mitigated by cost. If you don't have the money budgeted for the extras, you can use fewer of them at the party or shoot the street empty. Don't forget that along with the rest of the cast and the crew, those extras not only have to be paid; they need transportation and they have to be fed. Which brings me to catering. If you are serving lunch at seventeen dollars a head to a seventy-man crew and fifty actors over a fifty-day shoot, that will run over a hundred grand. That's a hundred grand just for lunch. Sven Nykvist used to tell stories of shoot ing with Ingmar Bergman in Sweden, saying how the actors would come to work in wardrobe from home, and how the cast and crew would take turns making lunch. Whenever I stand in the catering line adding up what the day will cost, I always remember Sven saying that Liv Ullmann made great homemade soup.

The enormous cost of film production has led to a splintering in the industry, with big studio commercial films on one end and small independent art films on the other. Yet even with independent films often running over ten million dollars in recent years, it makes experimentation a costly and high-stakes financial game. It is the undeniable reality of these hard costs that encumbers and restricts the art of film. On the large film projects, the studios, bonding companies, and accountants indirectly make artistic judgments, based solely on the bottom line. On small independents, it is the shallow and empty pockets that make those artistic choices. Think about the

1990s, when hundreds of films written to be shot in the United States were actually shot in Canada solely because it was cheaper. A decision made by someone with a calculator, not a viewfinder.

Except for a rarefied few, directors are routinely told to one degree or another that there isn't money in the budget for something. Maybe it's another shooting day or money to build, or to go out of town, or that there is not enough in the budget even for something as mundane as additional extras. Big or small, there is always a budget, and even at fifty million there is some degree of compromise. It may be show business, but it's still business. Which means that to maintain creative control, the director has to choose where to spend and where not to spend money. Consider, for example, a scene that says "The countess answers the phone" (one-eighth of a page.) The director may envision two hundred extras in black tie, with a symphony orchestra in the background and a crane shot rising up two stories as she picks up the receiver, but he may be able to afford only an empty foyer, an insert of a black gloved hand, and a camera on sticks.

So if you are thinking low budget, what is the formula for keeping costs down? Go back to square one—the writer with the sharp pencils and blank paper. Write a script that is makeable for a price. Think small cast, and only a few locations. Think contemporary time period. Think low-tech, no stunts and special effects. Think about the shock and awe of a brilliant script, of brilliant dramatic performances, simple lighting, elegant camera moves. Then remember that even directors making big-budget films have to make creative choices within the confines of a budget. They have to make sure that they get the money up on the screen, where they want it. So if you chose to cover that scene where the countess answers the phone with a simple insert of a gloved hand, no extras in black tie, no symphony orchestra or crane shot, if that simple shot works for the story, you will have that money to use some-where else. But even with the most cost-conscious approach to shot design, even armed with the wardrobe from home and a pot of Liv Ullmann's soup, to finance a feature film we're still talking private equity firms and investment banks. We're still talking about millions of dollars. We're talking calculators and viewfinders and the unfortunate truth that the art of film, no matter what the budget, is always mitigated by the art of compromise.

21

FIFTY-THREE SHOOTING DAYS. NOW WHAT? HOW TO SCHEDULE A MOVIE.

WHERE do you even start?

Almost never on page one. For the simple reason that it doesn't make financial sense, feature films are not shot in continuity. The best way to think about scheduling a movie is to equate it to a large jigsaw puzzle. Each puzzle piece, a single scene in the film, now recorded on a cardboard strip. Imagine taking all of the pieces, all of those strips from the board, and dumping them onto the floor.

The only way to begin a schedule is to start with a single hard fact. Certain things like an actor's schedule, the availability of a specific location, the night work—anything rock-hard and immovable—and work off of that. Sort of like finding all the straight-edged pieces of a jigsaw puzzle and creating the border. It is something definitive that hems you in.

For example, perhaps you know that the leading man is not available after September first, or that the seven nights have to be filmed back to back, or that the exteriors have to be shot before the season changes. Or that a specific location like a courthouse or school is available only on weekends. Shooting a scene at the Macy's Thanksgiving Day parade like we did on *Broadway Danny Rose*? That parade is happening only at 10:00 A.M. on Thanksgiving morning. Those floats will pass by only one time and you get only a couple of takes. Shooting at the ocean's edge for *The Prince of Tides,* for *Great Expectations,* or for *Evening?* Those tide charts are etched in stone. Shooting at a Rangers game, the Waldorf-Astoria lobby, an airport terminal, or a restaurant? A lot of locations and events have locked-in time frames that the film's schedule must accommodate. Think of these factors like the straight edges of the schedule puzzle.

Then move on to the wavy-edged pieces of the puzzle— the interlocking of actors' spreads. While the principal actors usually have a "run of the picture" deal, meaning that they are paid a flat rate to be available for the whole shooting period, actors in supporting roles, who may only be needed sporadically or for a certain block of time, may be on a daily or weekly contract. When scheduling, you have to consider which actors you can consolidate in a cost-effective manner. Obviously, it is cheaper to a pay an actor for two weeks than for ten or sixteen. There are so many maddening and conflicting union rules that scheduling a movie can begin to feel like an exercise in abstract logic. For example, the Screen Actors Guild has a "drop and pick up" rule for actors, which has a significant impact on scheduling. If you need an actor for just three days of the film, the drop and pick up rule states that if an actor works one day, you can drop him for ten days and then hire him for another day without paying him for all the days in between. But you can do this only once. Therefore, if you drop an actor but will need him again for additional work, even if that is only for a day, you will have to pay his rate for all the intervening days, even though he is not working. If an actor works on day one, day twenty and day fifty, it is going to cost a lot more (twenty-one days' pay) than if you can schedule the actor to work on day one, day twenty and day twenty-one (three days' pay.) Now multiply this equation by the sixty or so actors you may have in a film and remember that actors work together in scenes. Moving one day's work to tighten the spread of one actor may have a ripple effect on other actors' spreads. Think a five-thousand-piece puzzle, all in one color, or a game of pick-up sticks, where a single move can create a catastrophic tumble.

Just as with a jigsaw puzzle, to piece together the schedule of a film we try to group together all the scenes at a single location. In other words, if we have five days of work at an apartment, we schedule those days sequentially. Which, by the way, does not necessarily mean they are contiguous scenes in the script just because they are in one location. By consolidating scenes into a "block shoot," we are maximizing the efficiency of both time and money. It reduces equipment load-in and load-out time as well as location rental fees. Since each scene and each location has different requirements, where and when we are shooting becomes significant for all departments as information is disseminated and the schedule is set. The location department will have to make a deal with the owner of the apartment and the building, as well. Designers and set decorators have to have that apartment "dressed"— painted and decorated—by the shooting date. Grip and electric may prerig for lighting. The wardrobe and props needed for those scenes will have to be ready on that date. What are the transportation needs? What about dressing rooms, motor homes, parking, catering? Any special permits or equipment? What about generators, crowd control?

In addition to block shooting by locations, there are other general bylaws of film scheduling. We try to shoot the exteriors first, going inside to a cover set only as necessitated by inclement weather. That way, we won't get caught without the exterior work done at the end of the shooting period, when we might be hit with a couple of weeks of rain. Next we schedule any night work, back to back, in blocks just like for locations. Or if there are only a few nights, we schedule them on Fridays because we can't lose a day for the crew to turn around. We also try to save big, tough, emotional, or pivotal scenes for the end of the schedule, so the actors will have time to develop and better understand the characters they are playing. Built sets are generally shot last, so we can drop the motor homes, grip and electric trucks, and wrap any extra crew and equipment.

Someone experienced at scheduling a film also understands the dynamics of each scene and how it translates to time, taking into consideration such varied factors as a director's style, distance between locations, weather, wardrobe, and makeup requirements. If an actor needs to be aged thirty years for a scene, as Kate Nelligan was in *The Prince of Tides,* you have to schedule five hours into the day for her makeup alone. A move to a new location may take half a day. Rain effects add many hours to the schedule. Not only the time needed to set up the rain towers and do the street wet-downs but the time needed for the drying off of actors and costumes, and redoing hair and makeup.

The factors that go into scheduling are also interdependent. The fact that the diner you want to shoot in is available only until noon, or Woody has to be done by six on Mondays to play the clarinet, or that children can work only eight hours and actors need a twelve-hour turnaround—all wend their way into the equation.

Some decisions in scheduling are strictly financial. It's cheaper to consolidate actors' spreads, for example. Others are completely practical—say you can shoot at the school or courthouse only on a Saturday. Others are mandated by the reality of weather and seasons and sunlight. A handful revolve around artistic concerns. How a director wants to cover a scene dictates to a large degree how much time we need to shoot it. Even though the schedule and board are done very early in preproduction, adjustments are made when we scout locations and the director and other department heads weigh in with practical concerns and artistic choices. Questions like, "How about if we make it rain? Can we get a crane in here? Can we shoot it night for night?" (A scene written as night and actually shot at night.) The director cutting new edges to the puzzle pieces as we shuffle the strips, as we pencil in the time to manipulate the weather, go to a night call, move in a crane, adjust for actor availability . . .

Filmmaking is a business of exceptions, built on the rough assumption of the average: average page count, average number of shots. So how do you schedule a movie? Where do you even start? While it will almost never be on page one, it will always be with the hard, straight edge of a single fact, with the practical and financial boxing in the drama and the art.

22

SHOOT A SHORT DAY.

AFTER determining that the calendar adopted by Julius Caesar in 46 B.C. was out of step with the solar year, on October 4, 1582, Pope Gregory XIII created the Gregorian calendar and decreed the next day to be October 15. Ten days instantly vanished.

Filmmakers, it seems, are still looking for them. Sometimes we're just looking for a few hours so we can catch up on sleep. But most of the time we're looking for an extra shooting day, or an extra hour or two in each day so we can finish our work. Yet no matter how many times we try to find some extra time in the schedule, there are still only twenty-four hours in a day. It seems that even a single extra hour, let alone ten full days, is just impossible to ferret out.

Most film companies aim to shoot a twelve-hour day. But twelve hours often turn into thirteen or fourteen. Once a film crew works past eight hours, they're paid time and a half, and if they work past twelve hours, they're in double time. If the workday reaches hour fourteen without a break for a second meal, the crew is, because of penalties, effectively in triple time. Yet the producers are paying for these extra hours with more than just their checkbooks. Just like Pope Gregory XIII, a film crew working twelve or fourteen hour days finds itself facing turnaround—The film business's version of the disappearing day.

The Big Picture

While there is a confusing array of contracts and union rules regarding turnaround, I'll stick with the basics. For starters, turnaround is a union guarantee of ten hours between the end of one shooting day and the beginning of the next for the crew, and twelve hours for the cast, sometimes portal to portal, which means time is clocked to and from the actor's hotel, not the set.

Let's assume you're on location and it's day one and you bring in your crew and principal actors at 7:00 A.M. You shoot twelve hours and wrap at 7:00 P.M. The actors get back to their rooms at 8:30 P.M., after an hour to remove makeup and wardrobe and a half-hour ride to the hotel. They now have an earliest possible pick up at 8:30 A.M. the next day. You repeat the same thing on day two. The actors work twelve hours, take an hour and a half to clean up and travel, and are now home at 10:00 P.M. The earliest pickup on day three is 10:00 A.M. Day four's pick up would be at 11:30 A.M. and day five would be one o'clock in the afternoon. It is only week one of shooting, and already a Thursday and Friday morning have disappeared.

If you run the same numbers, assuming you work a week of fourteen-hour days instead of twelve, Monday's 7:00 A.M. call leaves you with a 3:00 P.M. call on Friday, and assuming that Friday is also a full fourteen hours, you are wrapping at 5:00 A.M. Saturday. This also means that for the second half of the week, you can't be scheduled for day exterior shots, because the bulk of your workday will be in the dark.

Now, you technically didn't lose those days; you still can shoot for the twelve or fourteen hours. It's just that you lost daylight hours, and depending on what is scheduled, you could find yourself trapped by turnaround in late calls, with your scheduled work impossible to shoot. You can juggle the schedule around, staggering actors' calls if possible, as you scramble for something to shoot, or head to an interior cover set that you should be saving for inclement weather. Just bear in mind that if the schedule says "exterior day" and your call is at three o'clock in the afternoon, that work can't be accomplished.

In addition to long days wreaking havoc with a film's schedule, there is also the cost of overtime to factor in. Consider that a straight day is eight hours, plus an hour for lunch. The next three hours are clocked at time and a half and after that in double time. If hour fourteen isn't another meal break, the company is forced to buy a meal penalty, which means paying an extra half hour at the prevailing rate (double time) for each half hour worked until the crew breaks for dinner. What all this means is that when you shoot a single fourteen-hour day, you pay for just over two straight days. And those extra hours are when the crew and the cast are fatigued and not necessarily giving a peak performance.

A five-day week of fourteen-hour days means you paid for just about eleven straight days of wages. By calculating man-hours, you got eight days of work condensed into that five-day week. All of which means that because of the premium wages, you paid for three days you didn't get to shoot. Over a twelve-week film that would be thirty-six days of labor paid for and not shot. Once again, it starts to feel just like October 15, 1582.

By shooting a short day, as we always did on Woody's films, generally about eight hours, we were able to prevent turnaround problems completely. We were able to stick to the schedule as planned, pay little or no premium wages, and have a well-rested cast and crew.

Obviously, I've simplified things a bit here. Shooting longer days shortens the shooting schedule and lowers equipment and location costs, and there certainly are times when it is financially sound to push through and shoot those twelve- and fourteen-hour days. Perhaps there is an issue of location availability, or by contract an actor has to be wrapped by a certain date, or the work to set the scene up (for example, shutting down and lighting the Brooklyn Bridge) makes it prohibitively expensive to leave and come back. But on a well-scheduled film, these long days should be the exception, not the rule.

Very often, the same studio that won't give you a few extra shooting days is signing off on enormous overtime and is more than paying for extra days by buying those expensive hours. I equate shooting long days with buying something because it is on sale and then paying for it with exorbitant credit-card interest.

There is no question that everyone scheduling a film, everyone driving home after a twelve- or fourteen-hour day, and every director who has ever shot a movie is looking for at least one or two of Pope Gregory XIII's lost days.

Ironically, by routinely sticking to an eight-hour shooting day, it was Woody who found them. He keeps the cast and crew rested, avoids the turnaround issue of disappearing days, and all the money he saves by not paying for those expensive overtime hours buys him extra shooting days. Remember that a five-day week of fourteen-hour days costs the same as eleven straight days of wages. These found days would appear on Woody's shooting schedule either as extra days of principal photography or in the form of reshoots.

While there is no denying that the financial formula for budgeting and scheduling a film is complicated and mitigated by issues of actor availability and equipment and location rental costs, all the production companies that think they don't have the money for extra days should consider shooting a short day. They might find those extra days they think that they can't afford, in all the money they don't spend on double time, triple time, meal penalties, extra lighting, lost locations, and daylight.

23

BLOCKING IS OVERLOOKED AND UNDERVALUED.

WRITING, casting and performance, shot selection and lighting, the lens on the camera, location and set design, and music and editing are the most obvious component parts of a film. Suspense, comedy, and drama are all built into a scene by the manipulation, the systematic layering and measured interplay, of these individual elements. Yet film viewers, and even film directors, often ignore the significant impact that the blocking of a scene can have on building suspense and drama or facilitating comedy. Most film viewers don't know what blocking is, and many film directors undervalue its overall importance by letting the actors overparticipate in the blocking of scenes.

Blocking is the process of choreographing a scene. Of deciding where the actors will sit and stand and how they will move, where they will be when they deliver their lines, and what their spatial relationship to one another will be. It is the planned integration, the melding, of the physical environment of the set with the actors themselves.

How each scene is blocked has a dramatic effect on both the rhythm and the timing of a film. An actor who walks to a distant corner of the room to deliver a line may add ten seconds of empty space to the shot. An argument that occurs face-to-face creates a different dynamic on the screen than one in which the participants are standing far apart. An actor who is sitting in a chair and yelling is less threatening than one who is standing nose-to-nose with, or moving in the direction of, an adversary. These choices of where the actors will be in relation to the set, to one another, and where they are in the space when they deliver their lines and perform any specified action (in other words, the sum total of how they move within the scene) is called blocking. And it should be done by the director. Yet many directors begin the blocking process by bringing the cast onto the set to experiment and see what "feels right" to them as actors. This approach is flawed and can undermine the director's role in the filmmaking process. As collaborative and as participatory as filmmaking is, the fragmented nature of the way films are shot mandates the consistent application of creative control on all facets of the project by the film's director.

The blocking of a scene is so significant because it impacts on the key creative issues of timing and drama and suspense, but also, in part, because it is integral to how a scene will be photographed. Blocking is the critical last step before the shot is designed. In essence, blocking is the final blueprint for how the scene will actually play.

To start, most directors walk through a scene with the actors, making suggestions as they go along. For some scenes, this is easy. For example, when filming a restaurant scene in *City by the Sea* with Robert De Niro and Frances McDormand, the script called for them to be seated at a table for the entire sequence. Blocking complete: They merely sat there. Conversely, in *Glengarry Glen Ross,* we had a scene in the real estate office with Al Pacino, Alan Arkin, Jack Lemmon, and Ed Harris that could have been blocked in any number of ways. Each of the actors could have been seated for the duration, as in the restaurant scene in *City by the Sea,* or the scene could have been blocked with a wide variety of combined moves about the room by the four actors.

94

BLOCKING IS OVERLOOKED AND UNDERVALUED.

Many directors, when blocking, pretty much give the set to the cast. They may say, "Why don't you both start seated here and let's see what happens . . ." The actors then start moving around, getting up to pace when it seems comfortable, and deliver their lines as they feel them. At any point, the DP may jump in and suggest that one actor not cross all the way to the other side of the room because it will add an hour to the lighting or will lead to a less than favorable shot composition.

Once the blocking is determined, the department heads are brought in, and the cast walks through the scene at half speed. Anywhere one of them sits or stands is marked with tape on the floor, which is color-coded and numbered, so that all the actors know where their positions one, two, three, and four are. The cast is then sent off to makeup and the crew lights the set.

That scene from *Glengarry Glen Ross* ended up with fourteen different cues for actor and camera movement. To block that scene took nearly an hour and was a result of not only the expression of director James Foley's concept but also of significant input from the cast and the cinematographer, as well.

It is only after a scene has been blocked that the angle from which the master (the whole scene in one take) will be shot is determined. The angles of all other covering shots (medium two-shots, close-ups, over the shoulders, etc.) will be based on the angle of the master and the actor's movement and eye lines within it. It doesn't matter if a room is being sprayed with machine-gun fire by a hit man, as we did in *F/X,* or we have Val Kilmer and Mira Sorvino seated on a park bench, as in Irwin Winkler's *At First Sight.* The process and the approach to blocking are pretty much the same.

An experienced director is preediting the film before it is even shot and will want to maintain control of the blocking. His task is to determine where each actor will be in relation to the others, as well as their size in frame. Should the camera move or the actors move, or both? How do you time these moves for the optimum dramatic or comedic effect? Are covering shots needed? The more experienced the director, the more precise his blocking will be.

Woody's approach to blocking is to not bring the actors to set at all. Rather, he decides on the shot with the DP, then lays it out with stand-ins. Once he is satisfied with the action and camera movement, and after considering the composition of the shots that will precede and follow the one he is preparing, the set is given to the crew to light. The actors have virtually no input in the process, unless some slight adjustment makes sense later. The key to this approach is that the randomness of how the scene will play physically has been eliminated. The actors are simply inserted into the equation later. Their opinions as to where to move or when aren't especially relevant.

Unlike directors who, when I ask them what they want to start with, answer, "I don't know. I haven't seen what the actors are going to do," Woody designs his shots based on his vision for the film. If an actor says he doesn't feel comfortable—say crossing to the window—the response is apt to be "Trust me. It looks great to the camera." This is the correct approach to blocking, because the director must execute his concept for the total film as we are photographing its individual component parts. A director should block based on how each scene plays against the connecting scenes, which may or may not have been shot already, as well as on how an individual scene contributes within the context of the overall film. By allowing the actors to participate in the blocking, a director is indirectly and subtly relinquishing a significant opportunity to keep control of the timing, pacing, shot selection, and overall dramatic tone of the project. Just because specific movement in one scene feels comfortable to an actor doesn't mean it will cut well with the bookending scenes—information the cast is not privy to. The line of demarcation where collaborative project meets director's vision should be clearly drawn. Actors should act; directors should block scenes.

24

THE BACKGROUND ACTION: HOW TO KEEP IT REAL AND WHY TO GET IT RIGHT.

FROM the pared-down requirements of a scene that calls for an actor to walk across an empty room and sit in a chair to the intricate and complex demands of a car chase through city streets, or crowds of extras at an airport, every single scene in a movie has to be staged. Staging involves not only the movement and actions of the principal actors but also the placement and timing of any and all of the background elements, from extras to motor vehicles, that will appear in a shot.

The most important aspect of staging a scene of course is the blocking, the choreography of the principal actors' physical action and line delivery. Once the scene is blocked, the director, working with the DP, must decide on the actual shot composition. The final element of staging a scene is the timing and placement of the background. There may be none, as in the example of an actor in an empty room, or it may be minimal—say just a pass-by of a single car or a few extras crossing in the background—or it may be elaborate—perhaps a scene that includes hundreds of extras and numerous motor vehicles with complicated background choreography.

Whether the scene's requirements are simple or complex, staging background is always governed by the same three tenets. First, it should look authentic, or the film loses credibility. Second, it should be done in such a way that it enhances and embellishes the scene, without being distracting. And third, the background should be choreographed in a precise and exacting way, because it will need to be replicated with the same elements and the same pacing in each take, and in each shot, so the coverage will match when the scene is cut together. For instance, the waiter arriving with the tray of drinks has to look authentic, not distract from the principal actors, and be timed to arrive at the same point the leading man delivers his line, and the woman at the next table asks for the check in every take and every camera setup if that is how it was originally staged. Otherwise, nothing will match when the scene is cut together.

While the director works side by side with the DP on the blocking of the principal actors and the shot design, it is the assistant director who stages and directs the background. On *Lovesick,* directed by Marshall Brickman, the script called for a funeral. We needed a hearse, limos, pallbearers, seventy-five mourners, and they each had to be placed and their actions staged. On *Arthur,* it was a wedding at St. Bart's church for director Steve Gordon. On *The Purple Rose of Cairo,* it was an elaborate 1920s nightclub scene with an orchestra.

But it's not just the big scenes that have background to stage. Every scene in every movie that includes more than the principal actors alone in a room has extras and background action to stage. I have staged thousands of scenes, and over 150,000 extras, in gang fights, restaurants, sporting events, prison riots, airport terminals, and hospitals. I've staged the background traffic patterns for busy city streets and complicated stunt sequences, background action for ordinary daily events, like an elementary school recess, and for not so ordinary events, like a death-row electrocution and a presidential assassination.

But how do you know exactly how to stage background? The script may just say a few lines about a motorcade and a sniper attack on the president or "Int. Operating Room," or "a nice wedding." Not a lot of detail.

To be good at staging the background action in a film, you have to be someone who is meticulously observant of ordinary human behavior. Someone who has a concrete visual conception of everyday events. Sometimes it's relatively easy. A hospital hallway, perhaps, or the hustle and bustle of an airport terminal—familiar-enough places. To stage background and re-create events for a film, you have to scrutinize procedure, becoming a recorder of the ordinary. A student of traffic patterns, dress, pacing. Look at the housewife with the two kids, the businessperson on the phone, the cab coming around the corner. How do they look? How do they move? Both the broad strokes and the nuance are important.

But what about those events that occur behind doors we normally don't pass through? How do you stage a prison riot? A case being argued before the United States Supreme Court? A rehearsal with the New York City Ballet? Eye surgery? Events outside the sphere of normal human experience can be a challenge. How many guards would rush into a cell block in a maximum-security prison during an uprising? What weapons would they be carrying? What is the protocol? You need to become a student of the extraordinary.

I've observed ocular surgery at Manhattan Eye, Ear and Throat Hospital firsthand. I've met with wardens, discussed Supreme Court procedures with constitutional lawyers, interviewed federal marshals and state police. Gone over the mechanics for electrocuting a man on death row with prison officials, and scouted morgues to review procedure for viewing bodies. I've done all of this so that I could get it right on film. How do they look? What do they do? Who else is around? What does it feel like to be in that space? What we stage and shoot has to look and feel real, or we lose the viewer and the film loses credibility.

When staging complicated scenes, we sometimes bring in technical advisers to be on the set and make sure that we get it right. Shrewdly, sometimes we even cast them to play a small role. A real federal marshal knows exactly how to handcuff and shackle a prisoner. For him, this is an ordinary activity. For us as filmmakers, casting an expert guarantees authenticity. Floyd Abrams, the renowned constitutional lawyer, was brought in to advise about Supreme Court procedures on *Nothing But the Truth,* and was cast to play a judge. In *Broadway Danny Rose,* Leo, the deli man from the Carnegie Deli, played the deli man from the Carnegie Deli. You can't get more real than that.

So before you stage a funeral or a big church wedding or a hospital hallway, pull from your reservoir of life experience. But if you have to stage something from beyond your realm of firsthand knowledge, get some advice. What you are looking for may be behind the closed doors of some of those places ordinary people often don't get to see. A prison holding cell, a newspaper editorial room, the stables at a racetrack, a shrimp boat, a live operating theater. Then abide by the three tenets of staging background. First and foremost, make sure it looks and feels authentic. Then stage each scene in such a way that the background is not distracting from the principal actors. And finally, make sure that the background is orchestrated in a way that it can be replicated with precision in all of the coverage for each scene so that it will match in the editing room and up on the screen. Keep it real and get it right.

25

MATCHING FOR CONTINUITY: WHY IT'S CRITICAL.

EVEN if we were to shoot a film in continuity, beginning on the first page of a script and filming each scene in order until the end, matching would still require meticulous attention. First we would have to match for screen direction (eye lines). The direction each actor looks, relative both to the camera and to each other actor in the master shot, has to be replicated in all the covering shots, so when the scene is cut together, each actor is looking consistently camera left or camera right within the scene. In addition to paying attention to the eye lines, as each covering shot is taken, spread out over the course of a twelve-hour day, we would have to match makeup, hair, and wardrobe. If an actress's hair is neatly combed in the master shot but in front of her face in the close-up, the two segments won't match and therefore one of them becomes worthless when it is time to cut the scene together. How about the amount of lipstick? How bouncy were this morning's curls? Was a shirt collar untucked in this morning's master shot but now, seven hours later for the close-up, is the shirt collar tucked into the sweater? How large were the sweat stains? How deep was the bruise? How wide was the puddle of blood? How about the level of liquid in a glass, or the length of the ash on a cigarette? Or the exact placement of the phone on the desk?

And how about the light? When we cut from this morning's master shot to the four o'clock close-up, if we are exterior the background light has to be adjusted so it will match. Cinematographers have to match not only light but also field sizes, camera height and movement.

The actors must also deliver a consistency of performance, in essence matching their mood and tone and their emotional level throughout the coverage. The script supervisor has to worry about everything, including making sure all the scripted lines were delivered in each take and in all the covering shots and that none were dropped or forgotten. The background extras and vehicles also have to match from camera setup to camera setup and take to take, not only which cars and which people but how they are timed.

Even if we were to pay attention to just the issues of matching within each scene and each shooting day on a film, it would require a constant and often frustrating focus for every department to get it right.

But films are not shot in continuity. Which means that in addition to paying close attention to issues of matching within each scene and each day, we must also throw into the equation the fact that we must also match for continuity days. Which takes the issue of matching to a whole new level.

We might have sixty shooting days in our schedule to film, say, eighteen continuity days and nights. (These are the actual days as written in the script.) When we factor in that we may shoot parts of several different continuity days on any single shooting day, or that characters may age several decades within the story, we have to be prepared with very precise information about the details of each scene. We may have three actresses in a single shooting day who require three different hair looks and corresponding makeup and costume changes because the scenes we are shooting are from different continuity days. On top of that, six weeks ago, when we shot the preceding scene, we may have had rain; therefore, the amount of water on the clothing and hair matters, as does the exterior light. (A cloudy day is needed or at least hoped for.) If we're exterior, roads may have to be wet down with fire hoses and rain may have to be made. In fact, two scenes shot six weeks apart may occur only a few seconds apart in screen time— the amount of time it takes for an actor to get into a cab and drive away, then subsequently arrive at a different location. We have to remove the real-time passage by matching for continuity. How tall was the grass? What color were the leaves and what was the quality of the exterior light six weeks ago? Because for our actor in our scene, again, only a few seconds have passed.

Every department has continuity issues, or matching, to consider—within each scene, between scenes, and within continuity days, as well. From matching light and seasons to haircuts and props, from emotional tenor to the thickness of accents, a scene that was shot a month earlier and the one that will be shot in three weeks, all have to have a level of consistency. The correct earrings, coats, ties, and shoes must appear and reappear on each continuity day. But also, that shirt collar that had to match from the morning to the afternoon, also has to match across the weeks and even months between continuity days. If we shot a scene with an actor arriving at a door three weeks ago, in today's scene of the door opening, our actor has to be in the same clothes, have exactly the same length hair, and be holding the flowers in the same hand they were in when he arrived on the steps three weeks ago.

Now multiply these issues by perhaps sixty actors, and fifty locations, and you can begin to see the magnitude of what matching means. Was the man who was shot four weeks ago in scene nine as bloody as he should be today in scene ten? In fight scenes, matching blood and bruising is often a nightmare, which is why we try to shoot stunts in continuity, as we did in *Hide and Seek* when Dr. Goodman (Robert De Niro) beats the sheriff (Dylan Baker) with a shovel.

If there is a game of billiards in a scene, all sixteen balls have to be reset to an exact spot for every take and new setup. Something that could be required dozens of times. For a dinner scene, the props must constantly match the level of food on every plate for every take. In *Lovesick,* John Huston had to carve a fresh roasted goose in each of five takes because they all necessitated starting with a bird right out of the oven. When Mira Sorvino and Val Kilmer ate hot dogs on a park bench in *At First Sight,* the props department went through well over a hundred hot dogs, so that for each camera setup there was a matching, partially eaten hot dog.

When we're losing the daylight and a wardrobe assistant is worried about the knot of the necktie on an extra in the back who's out of focus, it would be foolish to hold up the shot to adjust the tie. But for everything else, for everything readable by the camera, anything short of meticulous attention to detail will result in either a poorly crafted film or a whole lot of unusable footage.

26

WORKING BETWEEN THE SHEETS: THE ONLY THING "HOT" IS THE LIGHTS.

IMAGINE you are in bed, nearly naked, with someone from work. There are a least a dozen of your coworkers in the room, including a boom man with a microphone just inches above your head and a camera operator looking with a critical eye through a Panavision camera with a 20-mm lens just inches from your thighs. Now imagine that this is take six, you hate the person in bed with you, and you have to conjure up enough passion to light up the big screen. Sound romantic?

There are a lot of adjectives and descriptive phrases that come to mind when I think about shooting love scenes, and *romantic* would be at the very bottom of the list. In fact, it wouldn't even make the top fifty. While it may be well over a hundred degrees on the set, it's not sexual tension that generates that heat. All that high voltage is coming from a hard line to a generator and any rise in temperature is a by-product of the lights. That two-and-a-half-minute megawatt love scene you see in the theater probably took twelve grueling hours to shoot. Most of that time was spent on the technical requirements of getting the shot. The mundane start and stop nature of shooting coverage—the master, the close-up, the reverse—the equipment moves, the touching up of hair and makeup, and the matching for continuity amount to an automatic damper to any smoldering flame. Her lipstick, the exact placement of his shirt, and the topography of the sheets become the focal point of the day. All the energy is built in the editing room months after the actual scene was shot. The ambience provided by the mood-enhancing music is added during postproduction, as well. The truth is, in a love scene, the only one being seduced is the viewer sitting in the theater.

So what are the words that best describe what it's like shooting scenes where all of the action occurs between the sheets? *Tough day* might come to mind first. Followed perhaps by *pain in the ass*. Actors are rightfully concerned about cellphone cameras and unsavory pictures finding their way onto the Internet or providing an unprofessional chuckle at lunch, which adds one more layer of stress to the day. Or even worse, the very real concern about the paparazzi with telephoto lenses out on the street or on scaffolding down the block, zooming in for a tabloid cover from outside the window. While we try to block their view from strategic angles, we can't black out all of the windows because we light from outside as well as from inside the room.

Close quarters comes to mind even though the crew is stripped down to bare bones when we are actually ready to shoot the scene. But even with everyone not absolutely necessary on the set locked out, it still leaves a bit of a crowd. Think of it as you and your partner and a dozen or so very significant others crowded around the bed, providing criticism and suggestions. A sort of skeleton crew, up close and personal, manning the "closed" set, analyzing your performance from just about every angle. Not only photographing but recording sound to be played back in editing rooms and at dailies and studio offices, and not just the pretty, cleaned-up version with great lighting and music that we see in the theater but each and every take. Even with accessibility based strictly on "a need to watch basis," *overcrowded* certainly finds its way to the top of my descriptive list.

The Big Picture

Technical is also a good word for what goes on between the cinematic sheets, since shooting sex scenes mandates full body makeup with constant touch-ups. *Clearly defined* is aptly descriptive as we intermix body doubles with the real actors, as any nudity is contractually stipulated before an actor signs on to do a film. What body parts will be shown? And in what degree of undress?

Slow and boring also pops into my head, since sex scenes usually involve only two actors alone in a room. Generally, no extras or tough exterior locations. Usually, no stunts or props. Not exactly a strenuous production day. *Uncomfortable* and *awkward*, come to mind, more so for some scenes and some actors than others.

Perhaps *logistical nightmare* would be a good descriptive phrase for the scene in *The Devil's Advocate* in which Keanu Reeves makes "movie love" to Charlize Theron while fantasizing about another woman (Connie Nielsen). A scene that required interchanging the women as each camera setup was done and then keeping the two actresses separated as a way to help them stay in character and prevent one from seeing the other's performance.

Logistical nightmare would probably be followed by *comedic*—think Woody Allen in his underwear whining and it's pretty hard not to laugh. Or Nick Nolte, who was supposed to be wearing bicycle shorts under the robe he wore before crawling under the sheets, providing a good laugh when he went "commando" instead and flashed some of the crew on *The Prince of Tides*. Or Ashley Judd and Greg Kinnear asking for tips on *Someone Like You*. Or a particularly well-humored British actress during an awkward moment, which she immortalized by blurting out to the camera operator, "I hope you didn't see the royal beaver"—a laugh which found its way onto crew t-shirts the following day. A picture of a beaver—think big teeth, flat tail—carrying a scepter and wearing a crown.

Tough day, pain in the ass, boring, technical and logistical night-mare might not be the words you would conjure up when you think naked actors and sex scenes. Nor are they the words we hope you think of when you see these finished scenes in the theater. But those are the words that are listed in the filmmaker's thesaurus next to *nudity* and *sex scene.*

Clearly, for some actors it's body doubles, blacked-out windows, and a lot of stress, and to others nudity is "just another costume." But honestly, to the crew, it's "just another day" where the phrase "hot and bothered" has more to do with the temperature of the lights than with erotic notions, and where "long and boring" might best describe the day.

THE WISDOM OF THE
UNREHEARSED SCENE.

27

DURING the years I helped coach my son's soccer team, I was always urging players to "go to space" and be creative with the ball. Unlike football, which is extremely regimented and all about specific assignments and perfect execution of set plays, soccer is about creativity, instinct, fluidity, and thinking on your feet. The two games are polar opposites in terms of preparation and execution.

Whereas a professional football player has to memorize a playbook the size of the Manhattan Yellow Pages and be able to perform a very specific assignment once the ball is snapped, a pro soccer player can be traded to another team and play comfortably the following day. The game is *the game*. There is no playbook to learn, and the greats, from Pelé to Zidane to Beckham, have their value measured by their spontaneity and creativity. When the ball is on their foot, they run with it.

The divergent styles of directors' approaches to rehearsing and directing actors are not unlike the dichotomy of these two sports. Some directors appear to be playing football, where the actors are, through extensive rehearsal, learning "set plays." On most feature films, there is a rehearsal period, which usually occurs during the last two weeks of preproduction, a time when the actors can learn the director's "playbook." Yet some directors, like Woody, have no rehearsal at all. They appear to be

110

playing soccer; on the day of shooting, they just let the actors run with the ball.

So how does it all work? Why would some directors have extensive rehearsals and others none at all? For starters, it helps to understand the rehearsal process. While every director has a different approach, generally, even before a role is cast, the director has had discussions with each actor about his vision for the film as a whole as well as for each specific character. These discussions are broad-stroke and philosophical, but ensure that at the very least, everyone is on the same page.

Many weeks later, after the film has been cast and at the start of the rehearsal period, these discussions continue and the director gets more specific, fleshing out the elements of a character that are most important to him. It also becomes an opportunity for cast members to agree, disagree, or offer insights of their own. A good deal of time is spent on character. Will the actor gain thirty pounds, as Charlize Theron did for *Monster,* or get rail-thin, as Tom Hanks did for *Castaway*? On *Just Cause,* Ed Harris began the transformation to a psychopath on death row by shaving most of his head and adding some prison tattoos. Keanu Reeves, on *The Devil's Advocate,* worked with a dialogue coach to help him with a Florida accent. Every role requires its own degree of preparation.

During the rehearsal period, several hours are set aside each day to work on particular scenes. The actors involved meet with the director to discuss the thrust of the material, and the level of emotion required, then read through the scene a few times to see how the dialogue feels. It is during this phase that lines or phrases may be added or dropped from the script. Actors may make suggestions as they get to know their characters and acquire a comfort level with what they might say or do in a specific scene.

Some directors get even more specific during this period.

111

They may "tape out" a set in a rehearsal space and put in a few pieces of furniture so the actors can get up and move around as they rehearse their lines. Sometimes the actors really get into it, but generally any elevated level of performance is held back.

Often, directors will want to rehearse on location if possible, as well. On *Someone Like You,* director Tony Goldwyn rehearsed a scene with Ashley Judd and Marisa Tomei at the diner in lower Manhattan where we were actually to film the scene a month later. Having a sense of the real place, crowded with diners and staff and replete with background dialogue and clattering plates, provided them with a very real sense of the environment, where their voice levels should be, and what distractions might naturally occur. This process was replicated with maybe eight to ten actors, each taking turns on various days working on different scenes in different locations.

Last up is a "table read." This means that the director will sit with the bulk of the cast as they read through the entire script, not for performance, but to gain a broader perspective of the film. The actors are often meeting one another for the first time, so they can now associate a face with the words on the page, and the director can get a sense of how everyone may interact. Often through the process of rehearsal, a real rapport and comfort level is established between the director and the cast.

By going through rehearsals, when the day comes to shoot, the actors have a handle on their characters and what the director wants from each scene. Similarly, when Giant's quarterback Eli Manning calls for a "slot left, X fade route on two," all eleven men on offense know exactly where to run, whom to block, and what the count is. But that's the football approach. Regimentation. Discipline. Exacting detail. Well-rehearsed plays.

THE WISDOM OF THE UNREHEARSED SCENE.

Working with Woody would probably seem more like playing with an all-star soccer team. There was no rehearsal period, no running of lines at the locations, no table read, but every "player" or actor arrived on set well trained. His method was to have some character discussion with the actors, do makeup, hair, and wardrobe tests, but then let things be. In other words, he cast top actors and he let them act. Or so it would seem.

For example, for the brothel scenes in *Shadows and Fog*, John Cusack, Kathy Bates, Jodie Foster, and Lily Tomlin weren't brought to set until we were lit and ready to go. Unlike most directors, Woody would block each scene with stand-ins, not the real actors. Then, once the cast was on set, he showed them where to stand, or sit, or cross, and we did a mechanical rehearsal for the crew (for camera and boom moves, etc.), then did the first take. The scene had not been parsed or rehearsed over the course of several weeks. Nothing was hackneyed or stale. The material seemed new, the reaction and interaction real, and Woody was able to hone and adjust the timing and pacing as he saw fit. Since he put a great deal of faith and trust in his cast and their talent and experience and didn't rehearse, a much more spontaneous exchange was occurring in front of the camera. This brought a vitality and energy to the scene that is often lost in more exacting, verbatim, arguably overrehearsed performances.

On the surface, by trusting the cast and their instincts, the director is essentially letting them do what they were hired for. Act. If they were off base, Woody would always pull in the reins and point them in the right direction.

But there is another, more subtle reason, not to rehearse the actors. A metaphorical "trick play." At first glance, by not rehearsing, it may appear that the director is surrendering control, that he is handing the power over to the actors. He hasn't spent weeks going over lines, working with the actors to develop the characters, so it might seem that he is forgoing opportunities to convey what he wants from them. But the opposite is actually true.

By not rehearsing, by designing the shot with the DP, blocking and lighting the scene before he has worked with the actors and with no rehearsals to pull from, Woody is, in effect, putting the shot first and forcing the actors to fit into his planned visual scheme.

When they arrive on set, the unrehearsed actors are a bit on edge. They have never done the scene before. Not with Woody, and not with the rest of the cast. They haven't had a chance to say, "My character wouldn't do that," or "I think I would be more comfortable by the window." Woody shows them where to sit, stand, cross, and turn. He is directing by *not* rehearsing the actors. As a result, he is maintaining control of the scene and the direction of the total project. It may look like he's playing soccer, that he just put Beckham into the game and stepped back, but he's really playing football. He's just not showing the cast his playbook.

It may be Michael Caine and Max von Sydow in *Hannah and her Sisters* "running with the ball," but every single thing that unfolds on Woody's set was put into play by him. By not rehearsing, as a director he's not "dropping the ball." He's running football's set plays, which just happen to look like spontaneous soccer moments. By creating the shot first and not rehearsing, he is not only keeping the performances spontaneous; he is maintaining control of the film. He is directing.

28

THE ACTOR'S DON'T ALWAYS HAVE TO BE IN FRAME.

IN *Bullets Over Broadway,* there is a scene where the gangster hit man Cheech (Chazz Palminteri) takes a rival goon down to the docks and shoots and kills him. Later in the film, he does the same thing when he wants to get rid of his boss's girlfriend, Olive (Jennifer Tilly). The car pulls up at night, we see the dock and the water, the victims step behind a barrier that blocks them from view, and then we see and hear a gunshot, followed by a splash. Cheech walks back to his car and drives away. The audience doesn't see exactly what happened, but we aren't left in the dark, either. It is perfectly clear that neither the rival goon nor Olive is still with us, even though we didn't actually see them murdered. There were no stuntmen, no special effects makeup, no bullet hits, no squibs. It was a literal and a metaphorical "clean hit." The mission was accomplished in terms of delivering the story point in a streamlined, inexpensive, and relatively simple shot. Fundamentally, the scene was blocked in an effective and efficient way.

But the scene was not staged this way for simplicity's sake. *Bullets Over Broadway,* although a period gangster film, is, first and foremost, a comedy, which required that the violence be handled in a stylized, almost comic book manner. As a result, the shot design for these "hits" enabled the scene to sustain the comedic undertones necessary for the film, precisely because they were so bloodless and the real violence occurred off-camera. Clearly, when shooting a film, the actors don't always have to be in frame and the action of a scene can occur off-screen, as well. It is a device that Woody uses quite effectively for all sorts of creative reasons, and not just to soften and take the edge off of a violent scene imbedded in a comedy.

In an early scene in *Interiors,* Mike (Sam Waterston) is sitting at the kitchen table in his apartment, dictating into a tape recorder, when the door buzzer sounds. Obviously annoyed by the interruption, he gets up and leaves the room to answer the door. As he does so, he walks out of frame as the camera stays on a wide shot of the room. We overhear his conversation with Eve (Geraldine Page) at the door but stay with the tied-off camera shot of the apartment. There is no coverage, the camera doesn't move, and for part of the scene the actors are completely out of frame (twenty-two seconds). The overall effect this has is to focus our interest on the dialogue. We have no visual distractions, and by blocking the scene in this manner, Woody directs the film viewer's attention in a concentrated way to the words being spoken.

In *Stardust Memories,* there is a visually striking scene in the hotel room at the beachside resort where Sandy Bates (Woody Allen) is attending an event. Although we can't see him, he is lying on the bed, talking on the phone with Isobel (Marie-Christine Barrault), begging her to come see him. The camera is in another room, looking in through the doorway to the bedroom, as we hear the phone conversation. After a few seconds of a beautifully framed still-camera shot of just the room, while we eavesdrop on the conversation, Sandy's hand and forearm fall into frame. It is an inventive and creative shot that is effective in capturing the emotional tenor of the scene, the casual, voyeuristic sentiment that defines the moment so well. Most directors would have done a close-up of

Sandy speaking, as well as coverage of Isobel's side of the conversation.

What is striking over and over again, is how effectively Woody, especially in his collaboration with Gordon Willis, uses blocking and shot design as a strategic element in visually portraying the essence of each scene. Woody and Gordon rarely resort to standard coverage, often use a simple camera shot (in this case a locked-off camera) in combination with exceptional framing, lighting, and blocking.

In *A Midsummer Night's Sex Comedy*, which was also shot by Gordon Willis, there is a scene upstairs in the bedroom where Andrew (Woody Allen) and Adrian (Mary Steenburgen) are engaged in a conversation about the state of their relationship. Here again, as in the shots in *Interiors* and *Stardust Memories*, the camera is locked off (unmoving). In this shot, just as in the shot in *Stardust Memories*, we see part of two rooms, but this time there is complicated and visually interesting choreography as the two actors cross in front of the camera and walk in and out of frame. They walk to a part of the bedroom we cannot see, or into and out of the bathroom. It is roughly a three-minute master shot; the camera does not move, there is no coverage, and yet visual interest is maintained by inventive blocking rather than by either camera movement or coverage and editing. As in the two previous scenes, at a certain point, neither actor is in frame, which is a device that, once again, actually heightens our visual interest and attention to the dialogue.

Perhaps the most daring use of the empty frame is when Woody and Gordon Willis turn the camera to a blank wall. Not the blocked view of an actor to soften the violence in *Bullets over Broadway*. Not the temporarily empty apartment when Sam Waterston steps out of frame in *Interiors* and not a still camera shot of the empty hotel room in *Stardust Memories*, or the temporarily vacant bedroom in *A Midsummer Night's Sex Comedy*. Just

The Big Picture

the camera holding on a shot of white paint. Think of that first scene in Sandy Bates's apartment in *Stardust Memories*. It's a long, moving master shot of Sandy interacting with various employees. Yet the best part of all is when absolutely nothing is in frame.

Just as a pause in a musical composition can be as important as a note, the empty screen, the blocked view, the fade to black can at times be a more effective visual device than a staged event. Woody Allen and Gordon Willis used the empty frame, a simple daring shot of a blank wall, as a cinematic pause, a break in the visual sequence of a film. They used it for its starkness, for visual interest, or as a single element in a very complicated shot, as a transitional device, and for its sheer simplicity and arresting effect.

29

CONSIDER STEALING SOME SHOTS.

I'VE been shooting films in New York for almost thirty years. I've locked up more street corners and shut down more avenues and blocks than I can count. When we want to shoot a "walk and talk"—a couple of actors speaking a page or two of dialogue out on a city street— or film actors emerging from a cab, we first get permits from the Mayor's Office of Film to commandeer a few city blocks. We then make deals with business owners, negotiate with co-op boards, and often "dress" the streets. Sometimes in period costume, as in Philip Kaufman's *The Wanderers* or Woody's *Broadway Danny Rose,* where every streetlamp and motor vehicle, every storefront, every parking meter and gum wrapper that would appear in a shot had to be "period."

When shooting live on the streets, regardless of whether the film is contemporary or set in the past, every single element of what we do is measured and deliberate. We set up a perimeter and hold back or reroute pedestrian and vehicular traffic. We erect rain towers and lighting cranes. We remove signs, replace awnings, fashion our own graffiti. It is a lumbering, methodical task set against the backdrop of a vibrant, fast-paced city. Every single thing you see on screen is designed, crafted, and executed with precision by the crew. Every passerby is an extra, cast and staged. Every vehicle ours. Every wisp of hair is coiffed, every prop hand placed.

The Big Picture

Behind our barricades when we shoot, there are thousands of eyes and thousands of stories. Some people just want to watch, others just to pass through, and some just want to break chops. We barter, negotiate, strong-arm, and dance with all of them. We've shut down Fifth Avenue and the George Washington Bridge, filmed the Macy's Thanksgiving Day parade, walked cows down the streets of SoHo, made it snow in July.

But there is another way to shoot the streets. Forget the barricades and the set dressing. Let the traffic flow. Don't shut the city down; turn it up a notch and jump right in. In other words, *steal* some shots.

It is exactly what it sounds like—clandestine, exciting, completely unpredictable. It has the potential to backfire and is fraught with the possibility of getting "caught." So why do I love it so much? Probably because it is so clandestine, exciting, and completely unpredictable. Or perhaps because it is so seemingly impossible yet so easy. Like watching something predictably sluggish suddenly hit warp speed.

How do we do it? Just hide the camera, put the actors out there with wireless mikes, and roll. George Burns and Art Carney took a stroll down Fifth Avenue in *Going in Style;* the camera fitted with a long lens and hidden in some painter's scaffolding. Sydney Pollack, Judy Davis, Mia Farrow, and Woody Allen "walked and talked" down Columbus Avenue in *Husbands and Wives,* with the camera mounted and hidden in the back of a pickup truck. Then we did it again when Sydney Pollack and Lysette Anthony exit the theater and argue about *King Lear.* As the camera car drove slowly in the lane parallel to the actors, we in effect shoplifted a scene from New York's richly stocked shelves. It is authentic, spontaneous, and uncontrived. A cinematic covert op. It is fast, and it is cheap. The crew trimmed down to a handful of members. No set dressers, perimeters, or extras. No setting of the background. Instead of paying for each and every Screen Actors Guild extra, those pedestrians on the street are free and fair game. Just a master shot in a single hidden camera setup and the scene is in the can.

The secret to making it work? Hide the camera, not the actors. A famous face can slip into the crowd and often go unnoticed in the current and flow of the streets. Columbus Avenue on a sunny afternoon? Madison Square Garden during a Rangers game? Put the stars out there; just never let the city see the camera or the lights. Don't lay dolly track, or use a Steadicam; rather, mount the camera in a pickup bed or the window of a shop and let your actors walk the streets.

While stealing shots doesn't work for a period movie, if you're shooting a contemporary film, New York provides a live and vibrant stage. A true slice of cinema verité. Any day of the week, any time of day or night, the set is built, the streets and sidewalks always teeming, and the extras have cast themselves. When it works, as filmmakers, it means we're getting something rich for free. Like putting one over on the city that never sleeps, or crashing an exclusive private party without getting caught. Don't be afraid to break away from the convention and mechanics of standard shooting. Consider stealing some shots.

A FILM IS A WORK IN PROGRESS. **30**

THE process of filmmaking is, by its very nature, both inherently collaborative and intrinsically slow. The finished film evolving incrementally from thousands of interdependent factors: casting, set design, shot selection and style, locations, music, editing, tone and emotion. Unlike the architectural blueprint for a house, which contains such precise measurements and exacting detail that two separate builders working independently would construct two identical structures, a script in the hands of two different directors would likely result in two substantially different films. A script is closer to soft, malleable clay then to hard stone, more vague direction than measured step. And because a film is shot out of continuity, it evolves literally before our eyes, yet metaphorically behind our backs. Imagine each scene as a small, random section of a larger canvas, created independently over many weeks and not assembled or seen in continuity until months later, when the film is cut together.

A film demands unwavering confidence and steadfast vision. It takes hundreds of skilled hands to craft. Yet, as exacting as one tries to be, the creative side of filmmaking is not a linear process; it is decidedly more fluid and serpentine than precise and direct. Each element contributes in a defining way to the final outcome of the project. From the broadest, most far-reaching decisions—whom to cast, whom to hire for cinematography and production design, where to shoot—to the refinement of the shooting style, the specifics of shot selection, the musical score, the nuance of character definition. From the interpretation of the philosophical underpinnings of the story, to the tedious and mundane daily decisions that flesh out a film, the specific wardrobe for a scene, the choice of one location over another, the color of the paint on the walls, the tone used by an actor for an individual line. . . . From conception to delivery, filmmaking is an evolutionary process, a sort of slow, creative ferment.

A film is, by definition, and from its inception, a work in progress. Some more so than others. Some projects more conducive to literal interpretation. Some directors are more likely to go by the book, to use standard coverage, follow the script in a measured and definitive way. As an extreme example, think about the uniformity of a television series, where different directors get hired to step in and work on individual episodes and adhere to an established style. Some films, too, are very close to the scripts from which they arise. The dialogue in *Glengarry Glen Ross* performed verbatim from the script. The story points concise. The interpretation quite literal. The script adapted from David Mamet's Pulitzer Prize–winning play and written by the playwright himself, performed with systematic, almost religious allegiance to his written words.

Yet every director shoots material that does not make it into the finished film. We may shoot hundreds of thousands of feet of film but only print the good takes, and ultimately end up with only a fraction of the total footage up on screen. The discarded film is the unusable takes and coverage, which are a by-product of the editing process. But we also invariably shoot entire scenes that don't make it into the finished film. The scene may just not work creatively in the way the director envisioned it.

There may be pacing or length problems that aren't evident until the film is cut together. Whenever I first see a screening of a film that I worked on, I am invariably surprised by which scenes didn't "make the cut."

On *Evening*, Lajos Koltai shot a scene in Greenwich Village of a flashback to Ann Lord (Claire Danes) meeting her first husband that never made it into the film. On *F/X*, it was a substantial portion of a car chase that was left on the editing room floor. On *Big*, it was a scene where Josh and Billy (Tom Hanks and Jared Rushton) buy a tuxedo. (Better to introduce the tux when Josh steps off the elevator at the party than to see it first at the store.)

The fluid and evolutionary nature of the filmmaking process is evidenced by the preponderance of rewrites. In pre-production, new script pages are often issued so frequently that we color code them . . . the green pages replace the blue pages, which replace the original white. Writers are sometimes brought in when we are shooting to refine dialogue that just isn't working, or to add a scene the director feels he needs to tie things together, or to enhance the story.

Stardust Memories is a film that moves in and out of time and place, taking the viewer from distant and distorted childhood memories, to a film within a film, to past events, and the immediacy of the present day. From outright fantasy to current reality, the viewer is invited to stomp around in the private inner world of Sandy Bates. If you compare the original script to what ultimately ended up on the screen, dialogue and scenes are substantially altered, often rewritten and revised. Actors ad-libbed. Whole scenes were added and deleted.

In one of the early scripts for *Stardust Memories,* the scene that follows Sandy's gaze out of the luncheonette window, where he has become disenchanted with the possibility of a life with Isobel (Marie-Christine Barrault) and her two children, was a cut to a suggestive scene with Dorrie (Charlotte Rampling) and another man and woman in a ménage-à-trois. Although we shot the scene as written, it never made it into the final film. The scene that occupies its place is the gift exchange between Dorrie and the young, and then the older, Sandy on the beach that begins with a shot of an elephant. A seamless blending of childhood and adulthood, of fantasy and reality, a perfect moment that removes Sandy from the imperfect moment he is living with Isobel in the diner. Yet not in the original scripted material.

In *September,* the story is far more linear; the film extracted from the script in a much more direct fashion than *Stardust Memories.* Yet after the film was cast and shot, Woody, unhappy from an artistic standpoint with the result, recast several parts and reshot the entire movie. From day one. In his mind, the film didn't work, and because it had been shot at a single built location it was, comparatively speaking, a film conducive to reshooting. The part of the mother had been originally played by Maureen O'Sullivan, but was recast and given to Elaine Stritch. Charles Durning's role of the neighbor was recast and given to Denholm Elliott. The role originally given to Chris Walken was recast twice. The part was given to Sam Shepard and we shot the first version of the film with him. Then, finally, Sam Waterston was cast in the role in the reshoot. *September,* a showcase for the intangible, the chemistry that evolves during production. A work in progress to the end. So much so, that when it was finished, we started again.

31

EXPENSIVE TOYS AREN'T ALWAYS
WORTH THE MONEY.

I wouldn't say I'm a disaster in the kitchen, but when it comes to cooking, Escoffier I'm not. Though my kitchen is a chef's paradise, with all the bells and whistles and accoutrements that any cook could hope for, I know enough to stay away from the Cuisinart, the immersion blender, and the block of knives that promise the potential for a trip to the emergency room. A few stitches in a thumb, a vat of soup splashed across the walls, more burns than I care to count—have all taught me to keep it simple.

Most of the time, all I need is a great recipe, some fresh ingredients, and only the most basic tools necessary for the dish I am preparing. The rest of the gleaming copper, spinning blades, and exotic utensils are best left in their places unless they are really needed.

Directors face a similar dilemma on a movie set. Maybe they've only done a few indie or low-budget films and they're anxious to bring out the expensive "toys." Maybe they have a closet full of Oscars and a truckload of money, so they have carte blanche. Maybe they've been watching Emeril too much.

Too often young or new directors talk about making "cool shots," spending a disproportionate amount of time contemplating elaborate crane shots and complex Steadicam moves, but not enough time is devoted to what the scene is about and the optimum way to film it. Questions they should be considering are: How much camera movement might be appropriate? What lenses should be employed? How many setups are necessary? What is the scene cutting to in sequence? What is important with regard to the emotional state of the characters? In other words, what is the scene about and how would it be most effectively shot?

Just as in my kitchen, there are a lot of tools available to the director on a set, but many of them are better off left for special occasions. Like me with an immersion blender, spraying a béarnaise sauce across the ceiling and wasting several hours cleaning it up, the director may decide to do a 360-degree Technocrane shot that will cost him five hours out of a twelve-hour day. But when all is said and done, he merely established a set and a few characters, which he could have done with a camera on sticks, and all I needed was a simple whisk. After lunch, he will now have only six hours to do the rest of the day's work, which invariably leads to compromise. He has done a "cool shot," but he now has only half a day left to shoot his 24/8 pages of dialogue, which is a full day's work. Because the whole filmmaking process is about money as well as art, the question becomes, Was the shot worth it?

With Woody there are inventive and interesting shots in all of his films. Yet I can't recall using a crane before *Shadows and Fog,* and I saw a Steadicam only once—on *Hannah and Her Sisters.* (After using it for a scene on Fifth Avenue after Mickey Sachs [Woody] exits the doctor's office, we actually reshot the sequence with the camera mounted on a conventional dolly.) Woody's innovative coverage comes from shot design, not expensive toys.

There are certainly a lot more toys available at the film-equipment rental houses than I have in my kitchen, and directors tend to overuse them. I've learned you don't need a candy thermometer to make tea, a stick blender for hot cocoa, or a Titan crane for a scene in a café. The key is knowing what to use and when.

The Louma crane has a telescoping arm and remote head that allow it to extend or retract and can rise twenty feet into the air. An Aquila crane can get up over a hundred feet. A Technocrane is also a telescoping crane with a remote head that can glide out over water (as we did on *Evening*), rise and swivel at varying speeds and heights, and is great to arm over a traffic jam on Park Avenue, as we did on *Click*.

The Titan II is a crane mounted on a truck that can drive on rough terrain, has wheels that can crab, and several options for arm height. The camera is operated conventionally by an operator and assistant cameraman, who are seated at the end of the crane arm and ride with it. Counterweights are used to offset the other end, where a grip can swing or tilt the arm as necessary.

Steadicams can glide up and down stairs, through wooded terrain, and peek around corners. There are crane arms mounted on insert cars, like the Shotmaker, which allow for very intricate moves while filming speeding automobiles. Aerial photography allows a helicopter to become, in effect, a huge dolly in the sky that can do myriad maneuvers at different speeds, angles, and elevations.

Though aerial photography is expensive, most of the other equipment mentioned is not when weighed against an average budget. Cranes with a technician can be had for a few thousand dollars a day, and generally a few extra grips are employed to assemble the equipment and set it up. But the expense is not the line item. Indeed, on bigger films, some cranes, as well as Steadicams, are rented and available for the entire shoot. The real expense is the time to block, rehearse, light, and execute the shot, and the subsequent effect that has on the rest of the day's work, including not only the number of setups that can be accomplished but also the number of takes that can be done and the quality of performance. The list of toys that enable a director to make a great shot is extensive, and the issue isn't just about time and money. It's about the art. Great shots are more often about design than equipment.

It might seem to be fun and innovative to use a Steadicam to cover a "walk and talk," but, in fact, doing the same shot on a conventional dolly will provide you with a smooth and uniform speed and a rock-solid frame line. Since the Steadicam floats and therefore is less exacting, it is much better saved for using on unlevel ground, going up stairs or slopes, wading through water, and so on. Places a dolly can't be used.

Do you want to spend five hours setting up and rehearsing with a crane, which by virtue of its size fills up a set, is hard to light around, restricts movement of extras and motor vehicles, and requires the precise moves of half a dozen crew members, or is there a simpler method of recording the same action?

When analyzing a scene, the question for the director should be, What is the scene about and how can I tell the story and embellish it without self-conscious camera moves? For as soon as the audience starts saying, "Wow, look at that cool shot," they are no longer listening to what the actors are saying. They've fallen out of the story and have been distracted by a mechanical aspect of filmmaking.

Sure, a helicopter shot of a car traveling over the George Washington Bridge, or a bus traversing a desert highway, is an effective use of equipment. But a crane for an interior to cover two people sitting at a restaurant bar talking? You are probably wasting a lot of time and money that would be better spent on additional takes or other material, and merely creating a self-conscious camera move.

The truth is, there is a lot of equipment available to filmmakers, and when used judiciously, it can be effective in providing innovative and dramatic shots. The trick is to know the equipment, its limitations and advantages, and the real time and cost to utilize it. Then ask the hard objective question: Is it right for the scene? With the right ingredients, you can make a great omelette with a balloon whisk and a simple skillet. And great shots are more often found in the director's head than in an equipment catalog. Know when the toys are really worth it.

32

DON'T USE A FLAMETHROWER
WHEN A MATCH WILL DO.

SOMETIMES filmmakers use the term *flame-thrower* as a derogatory reference to a cinematographer who overlights. Since lighting is both artistically critical and logistically timeconsuming, filmmakers constantly face the dilemma of needing to "get it right" while needing to "get it done." Suggesting in conversation that the DP is a flamethrower lets everyone know we will be moving slowly. Maybe lighting the bridges and tall buildings of the deep background for a scene that will be shot in close-up, or lighting the exterior streets of two city blocks when we are filming an interior. That the cinematographer will basically be using a flamethrower when a match would do.

On *Husbands and Wives,* there is a night scene on Park Avenue which called for Gabe (Woody Allen) and Judy (Mia Farrow) to be seated in a car at a traffic light, musing about relationships as they watch another couple cross in front of their car with an early edition of the Sunday *New York Times.* The scene symbolically pulls them back to an earlier, simpler time in their lives. Woody and Carlo Di Palma got the shot in about two hours at the end of a day, using the ambient light from a street-lamp along with one 10 K (a large light) on the roof of one of our trucks. Our normal complement of six electricians and six grips was more than adequate to accomplish the shot. It isn't necessarily a beautiful shot, but it didn't need to be, either. It is a scene that simply needs to communicate a story point.

On *Great Expectations,* directed by Alfonso Cuarón and shot by Emmanuel Lubezki, we filmed a scene where Finn (Ethan Hawke) emerged from the subway and crossed an intersection, heading toward the SoHo art gallery that was hanging his show. The script read "Ext. Subway—Night. ⅛ page" and on "Action," Finn climbed the steps, looked around, and crossed the street. Cut. One actor, no dialogue, not a big dramatic scene, just a utility shot, an eighth of a page of shoe leather. Yet for this, we used six manlifts for lights, two generator trucks, about eighteen electricians, and had a prerig for cable runs during the day. In fact, nearly two city blocks were lit. All this for about ten seconds of screen time (which, incidentally, never made it into the finished film). In this example, Carlo Di Palma in Woody's scene used a match, while Emmanuel Lubezki used a flamethrower. The question is, Was all the lighting time and money necessary to get Finn across the street worth it, and, conversely, was Woody making a compromise in his scene?

The short answer to both parts of the question is no. And not just because the scene from *Great Expectations* didn't make the final cut. On *Great Expectations,* the shot could have been smaller, with less elaborate lighting, and still conveyed a well-lit story point, and Woody's scene in *Husbands and Wives* was lit in keeping with what that scene needed to accomplish and wouldn't have been made "better" with more time and equipment. I've seen Sven Nykvist do more with light artistically using the bare bulb of a table lamp than what some other cinematographers accomplish with an open checkbook and a hard-wired line to a power plant.

But the statement "Don't use a flamethrower when a match will do" has a broader application when it comes to filmmaking. It applies not just to cinematographers and lighting;

but can be used to describe the overindulgent, misappropriated use of equipment and time across departments and throughout a film. I've worked on films that, as a routine, ran three to five cameras a day for interior scenes. Three to five cameras, not for an elaborate stunt, but merely for people in an office talking. I've spent six hours, half of a $100,000 shooting day, on a Louma crane shot that could have been accomplished with a dolly in a third of the time. Yet not using a flamethrower when a match will do doesn't mean that you shouldn't get those beautifully lit scenes or those time-consuming great shots that both Carlo Di Palma and Emmanuel Lubezki are known for, because you should. They can, and often do, define a film. It just means that you should know when to pull out all the stops and light those two city blocks, when to shut down the streets and bring in that crane, and when to just "get it done."

33

FORGET ABOUT THE MONITOR.

TELEVISION sitcoms are generally shot on videotape, with three cameras running simultaneously and the director sitting in a booth, watching and directing via a video feed to a number of monitors. The director effectively selects shots, chooses coverage, and edits as he watches the TV monitors as the episode unfolds, often before a live audience. It is standard practice for TV directors to work in this fashion, removed from the actors and the set, as the video and audio feeds stream onto monitors. This is common practice not only for live TV but for TV news, three-camera television, and live-action sports.

When you consider that there is virtually no artistic expectation surrounding the taping of the news or even a sitcom (when is the last time you saw a great shot on *Two and a Half Men* or an interesting shot on the evening news?) and that there is the irrefutable reality that the show will ultimately be broadcast on a TV screen just like the one the director is directing from, it makes sense. In fact, directing television while watching a monitor makes sense for a whole lot of reasons, from the budgetary restraints of filming a television series to the reality of taping live news and sporting events, and is ultimately justified by the fact that viewers will watch the show on a similar, if not identical, screen.

FORGET ABOUT THE MONITOR.

And when the technical capability became available to feature film directors to run a video feed from a 35-mm camera, and see either live or taped video playback of what they were shooting on film, many feature directors started directing movies while watching performances on a monitor. And I'm not just talking about the feature directors who come from the world of television, or first-time directors who may find comfort in a fifteen-inch screen. Francis Ford Coppola often directed from monitors while seated in the "the Silverfish," his Airstream motor home. Mike Nichols, Steven Spielberg, Bernardo Bertolucci—lots of world-class, well-known, and respected directors rely on a monitor.

Some feature directors use the video monitor as an effective tool, on an ad hoc basis, say to double-check complicated and expensive stunt scenes. The car-chase scene in *Just Cause* is a case in point. We shut down a major causeway going from Miami Beach to the city of Miami, ran thirteen cameras simultaneously, and had multiple stunt drivers enacting a precisely choreographed sequence that culminated in a jump over an open drawbridge at high speed. The stunt cost hundreds of thousands of dollars (the helicopter unit alone ran forty thousand), and video playback assured us that we'd gotten the shots we needed. We didn't have to do another expensive and dangerous take, because we were able to check the footage on the monitor. With the technology of the monitor and video playback, director Arne Glimcher was able to confirm this, not in dailies the next day, but right there out on the street before we wrapped for the night. This was technology being used to our advantage.

But cut to a dramatic scene between two actors and try to make sense out of the fact that the director is sequestered in a "video village," in a room off set, directing the scene while watching it on a monitor. Sort of like parenting through a video feed from your home to your office—you're guaranteed to miss a lot, and nothing beats being right there in the heat and fray. There is certainly no technical justification for it, and when you consider that the piece of footage you are directing from that television monitor will be projected onto a gigantic movie screen, and that every nuance in the actor's facial expression and performance will be magnified, it is hard to understand it from an artistic standpoint. It is worth noting that the actor's face, the details of the set, the subtleties of performance, which may be almost unreadable on that monitor, will be larger than life when projected onto the big screen, measured in movie yards, not television inches.

Woody's favorite spot? Right next to the camera. Monitors? Not in my tenure with him. Not even for *The Purple Rose of Cairo,* which had some split-screen shots and where we could have used a monitor to check on the technical details. Nor did he resort to a monitor on any of the films when he was acting in front of the camera as well as directing. Instead, Woody relied on his own instincts as a director and a performer, and on those of the professionals around him.

So use the monitor as a tool when mandated by necessity, not as a superfluous and handicapping crutch. Avoid the inevitable "direct by committee" tendency that evolves when you set up chairs around the monitor and random members from the cast and crew cluster around the TV screen in this makeshift video village, offering comments on performances and takes. Does a director want to have the actors looking over his shoulder at each raw, unedited performance, possibly making adjustments in the next take on their own, or losing confidence, concerned about how they look, or simply not understanding exactly how the director envisions this individual piece fitting into the totality of the film? Does Barbra Streisand really need to hear from Nick Nolte's driver what he thought of the most recent take? Probably not. And it certainly wouldn't happen if the director wasn't tethered to a video feed, but stood instead, trusting his instincts and vision, on a live set. Yet it happens all the time around a monitor. Most people are overwhelmed by the sheer magnitude and scope of a live movie set, but all of us feel like experts when seated in front of an ordinary television screen.

Does a monitor have its place on a feature film set? Sure it does. For complicated stunt sequences? Definitely. Use a monitor to check critical technical details. Then consider using one so the DP can check framing and as a protective measure for any shot where the director can't stand behind the camera, like a high crane shot. But don't take the technology that evolved out of the limiting constraints of television and apply it to the wide-open expanse of feature films. Don't condense a feature film to a television screen by choice. A feature-film director should stand behind the camera, not be isolated from the set. Remember that there is energy on the set, nuance to expression, details of makeup and clothing and gestures that will be missed on that fifteen-inch monitor but be very evident in the theater. There is spontaneous, personal interaction between director and actors, and fluid communication between the director and key members of the crew, when the director is on set that is lost somewhere along that video feed. So don't take a tool from television and apply it across the board to feature films. Remember that movies are shot, first and foremost, for the big screen, not for the "little box."

34

MOVE THE CAMERA.
THEY INVENTED THE DOLLY
FOR A REASON.

TO frame an argument for moving the camera, I could just list films and directors who utilize innovative moving-camera shots. Alfred Hitchcock in *Frenzy, Vertigo,* and *Notorious,* Orson Welles in *Touch of Evil,* Jean-Luc Godard in *Weekend,* Martin Scorsese in *Goodfellas,* Alfonso Cuarón in *Children of Men.* But there are just too many great moving-camera shots to even begin a comprehensive list. So instead, I could just state the obvious: that a moving picture preassumes a moving camera. And that moving the camera can be effective as a tool to build energy and suspense. That a moving camera can lift the audience from their seats and put them "in the moment" of the film. Or, depending on the shot, can go a step further and render the viewers more than distant and safe voyeurs by putting them "on the run." Literally. Through the hall and down the stairs and into the street in *Frenzy,* or in that car, transporting the future of mankind in *Children of Men.* I could state more of the obvious: that moving the camera can create a bracing sense of fear, that the moving-camera shot is a photographic device used to interject tension or simple visual interest, or both. Using by way of example the shot in *Shadows and Fog* where the killer is in the coroner's lab and the shot tracks behind the beakers, peeking through the glass, the camera symbolically stalking, the view partially obstructed, the camera moving in several simple dolly shots. The design of this camera sequence, the choice to replicate a stalking motion, instrumental in foreshadowing the possibility of a pending attack. The moving-camera shot, in this case, is visually interesting as it interjects tension.

But the best argument for moving the camera may be simply this: that the camera, in its role of telling the story of a film, should replicate, then optimally enhance our true-to-life visual experience. That in film, the camera becomes our eyes and its imperative is to not only make whatever it is photographing look as optically real as possible but also to make it look a lot better. Planned and edited. Color corrected. Visually perfected. And then I would simply observe that our real-life visual experience is not static. Our eyes move, we move, and the visual world around us moves. That we are soft-tissue Panavision and Arriflex. We are twenty-twenty and soft focus. Our real-life visual experience is comprised of long tracking shots, sometimes gliding like a Steadicam or forging forward on the wheels of a dolly, sometimes handheld and jittery. We may zoom in for a better look, adjust focus, pan across the room, turn around and get the reverse, pause for an establishing shot. We crane and tilt. We are dollying, steadicaming, zooming, panning, handheld, ocular human beings. Our eyes move. We move. And so should the camera.

In a well-crafted film, the most important job of the camera is to tell us a story by showing us the story the way we would visually experience it if we were right there. Only the camera must do it better. Just imagine that if in real life every visual experience, every turn or tilt of our head, was carefully planned. That before we opened our eyes to capture an image, to experience an event visually, we had the perfect shot composed, the best angles and the ideal coverage. Imagine that before any images reached our optic nerve and our brains, they were edited. Throw in perfect makeup, some great music, a little color correction, some well-executed camera moves, and you have film. And the very best films deliver, photographically, the optimum. And that requires well-crafted camera moves.

But the very best argument for why the camera should move is that the moving camera, the actual design of the shot, can, in some scenes, play a more significant role in building drama and emotion than any other element of the scene. That the emotion, the compelling story point of a scene, can be communicated not by what a character says or where the scene is shot, or by who is cast, but by how the scene is covered. By how the camera moves. I could demonstrate this just by referencing a single scene from *Great Expectations*: Alfonso Cuarón's long Steadicam sequence of Finn (Ethan Hawke) running through the streets of SoHo, as we follow him into a restaurant, through the bar to find Estella (Gwyneth Paltrow) in the back, seated at a table. Then after a brief dance with her, and without a single visible break in the film (there are actually three shots of him running prior to entering the restaurant that were seamlessly hidden), we follow them back through the bar and out onto the street for a kiss in the rain and a high crane shot as they walk away. Was this a self-conscious camera shot, chosen just because it was fun or cool? Hardly. The selection of the moving camera, beginning with the long tracking shot, followed by a Steadicam, then ending with a crane move, in exactly the way it was used, is precisely what the scene commanded. This scene could have been covered in any number of ways. And an inexperienced director might have chosen a more conventional approach. Perhaps an establishing shot of the restaurant, followed by cuts to a series of static shots. But it would have lacked the sophistication and the dramatic tension, and would have been the wrong choice.

Picking the right shot, knowing when and how to move

the camera, knowing what is the perfect choice for the scene, is part of what being a director is all about. And the camera should move when the scene will be enhanced by its very move- ment. Imagine a car chase being covered with a montage of sta- tionary camera shots. It is never done this way because it is a blatantly wrong photographic approach. We don't experience a car chase, or Finn's fierce determination and burning desire, in a visually static way. Both an automotive and an emotive "run through the streets" need aggressive motion and a camera that moves.

Great directors and great cinematographers are always looking for innovative ways to move the camera. Hitchcock did it in *Vertigo* with the zoom, Garrett Brown did it with the invention of the Steadicam, and Alfonso Cuarón's film crew did it in *Children of Men* with a specially designed car rig that could swivel the camera 360 degrees in the interior of the car, just to name a few. So move the camera for all the obvious rea- sons, for visual interest, to build energy and suspense. But then examine the script to see when and where the moving camera can be used in a more profound way. Find those shots where a moving camera can actually define and carry the scene. Where the shot itself eclipses every other element be- cause its very design is the perfect complement to the material. Take the audience on a run through the streets or on the ride of their lives.

35

THEN LET IT STAND STILL: VIRTUES OF THE STATIC CAMERA.

WOODY opens *Manhattan* with a series of fifty-five static shots before there is a single camera move. In putting together this sequence, he essentially establishes the physical set, the city of Manhattan. He chose to present it in the simplest of cinematic styles. A "locked-off" camera. Similarly, Woody opens the film *Interiors* with a stationary camera. In this case, seventeen cuts, most of them of the stark interior of a house and used, effectively, to establish the psychological stage, the emotional landscape, of the film. In both of these opening sequences, the camera does not move.

A locked-off camera shot can be used either independently, as in these montage openings, or it can work as just part of a shot, a stationary camera piece embedded into a longer shot embellished with camera moves.

Often, if the camera is stationary, locked off or "tied off," the actors are moving. Some of the opening shots in *Interiors* catch Mary Beth Hurt as she is seen crossing the room in the reflection of the glass on a painting, climbing the stairs, or walking into an empty frame. Actors moving in and out of the frame of a stationary camera is a signature Gordon Willis shot. He often designs shots with both elegant camera moves and a stationary camera, brilliantly combining a static and a moving camera in one stylish setup.

But what happens if the camera is tied off and the actors are effectively "tied off" as well, while the scene is covered in a single camera setup? No camera movement, no actors moving about the room, no coverage, no cuts. What holds the scene together? What gives it visual interest, adhesive grip, and energy? The shot composition? Of course. The lighting? Without question. Emotional content? Dialogue? Absolutely. But more often than not, in order for a stationary camera filming a stationary actor to hold audience attention, the scene must deliver a performance with enormous emotional heft. So much so that actor or camera movement would detract and diminish it. To justify a static camera and a stationary actor, the scene's energy must erupt from its very stillness.

Carlo Di Palma, an absolute master at moving the camera, demonstrated how good he was at keeping the camera still in the film *September* when he and Woody did just that; they used a stationary camera to shoot a stationary actor. Consider the riveting performance of Elaine Stritch in front of the bedroom mirror as her character, Diane, laments about her age as she speaks to the audience, as she speaks to her daughter, who is offscreen. The camera setup begins with a two-shot of Lane, played by Mia Farrow, and Diane standing in the bedroom. Then the camera follows Diane as she sits at a dressing table in a "single," where the camera remains stationary, moving only imperceptibly to adjust framing, as she delivers the soliloquy that begins with "It's hell getting older." She barely moves beyond what is necessary for breath and speech as the stationary camera peers at her reflection in the mirror. It is the best of theater, an actress alone on the stage, speaking to the audience. A little bit of Broadway in *September.* Nobody moves. Not the camera, not the actress, and not the audience.

Consider Elaine Stritch in the same film, this time on the couch in the living room as she laments about life, as she speaks to the audience, as she speaks to her dead husband. "Rap once if you hear me, Richard." We tilt up from a candle to her face and then once again, a static camera, a near static actress, a single shot and the audience is immobilized by the moment.

Woody also demonstrates the brilliant use of a static camera in *Stardust Memories*—in the scene where we see the character of Dorrie, played by Charlotte Rampling, at an institution. There is nothing on the screen but the falling apart, the complete deconstructed remnants, of Dorrie. Her mental collapse, captured in a series of still shots, enhanced by the irregular editing of jump cuts, the off-kilter unbalanced clips a demonstrative and effective device used to illustrate the emotional condition of the character. An absolutely brilliant use of cinematic techniques. Concept, performance, and editing trumping photography.

Or is it? In these instances is the simplicity of a stationary camera, photographing the close-up of the anguished face of Charlotte Rampling and her repeated fragments of dialogue—an ode to her insanity—not the best part of the scene? The tight close-up of Dorrie's face, complemented by the ragged cuts, creates a riveting series of images with the most basic form of film photography: a tied-off camera. Gordon's and Woody's version of point and click. The power of the scene, and the photographic style, as raw as the emotion up on the screen. Consider again the anguished reflections of Elaine Stritch in *September*. Is the photographic simplicity of these scenes the most brilliant move of all?

In each of these cases, the viewer is engaged by the performance, swept up in the compelling current of the scene. The locked-off camera gets our attention because the performance is big enough to take on the simplicity, the purity, the silence and stillness of a stationary camera facing a stationary actor head-on. When used in the hands of great directors and cinematographers, when used to simply and cleanly capture a significant performance, whether used with the brilliant editing of the scene from *Stardust Memories,* or in a single shot with no editing at all, as in *September,* a stationary camera and a stationary actor can bear more energy, carry more weight, than a complicated dolly shot, an elaborate Steadicam move or a swooping crane. Just the purity of a locked-off camera. The blunt force and impact of a cinematographer wielding a stripped-down, basic tool. A stationary-camera shot executed with enough force to visually arrest the audience.

36

THE ABSOLUTE BRILLIANCE OF THE SINGLE MASTER SHOT.

A scene in a film is usually assembled from a compilation of shots. You normally do a wide master shot of the entire scene first, which, in turn, dictates the coverage (the other shots you will use). A static or a moving master shot can also be utilized to cover an entire scene in a single camera setup, not to serve as *part* of the coverage for the scene, but as *all* of it. The shot may, effectively, include many of the same camera angles a director might get using standard coverage, which may require ten camera setups and a full day to accomplish. But by blocking and lighting the scene for a single master shot, the actors perform and the camera photographs them without a cut in the film or a break in performance. In other words, the actors perform the scene not in splintered parts, not over and over again as the director shoots lots of different angles, but in its totality as the camera traces a carefully choreographed and lit path around them. For example, the camera may start wide, push into a two-shot, pan to a single, then widen out again, photographing a number of different sizes and images incorporated into a continuous take. Or a scene can be shot as a single master, with a locked-off camera recording the carefully blocked movements of the actors in front of it.

While it is complicated and somewhat daring to block and light a long master shot, a scene designed and shot in this manner can save a lot of time and money because it completely eliminates the need for coverage. It also, to a large degree, eliminates the need for matching, since the director won't be cutting segments together. No need for the actors, the director, the script supervisor, or any department, for that matter, to be concerned about matching eye lines, extras, wardrobe, or makeup and hair within the scene. Further, covering a scene in a master shot, not as part of the coverage, but as the sum total of it, also gives the actors freedom to perform and deliver dialogue in a more natural way. They may overlap, step on one another's lines, ad-lib, and improvise without regard for matching to a previous take.

The single master shot also provides a great format for filming comedy. By covering a scene in one continuous take, the jokes, as well as the reactions to them, are presented in a single uncut format. Indeed, cutting back and forth within a comedic scene can cause the scene to run a little longer, which can slow down the pacing and timing.

An interesting facet of covering a lot of scenes in single master shots is that it mandates that the director preedit much of the film in his head. If you shoot lots of coverage, get every possible shot, then worry about how you will assemble each sequence in the editing room, you don't necessarily know, in a definitive way, what the finished scenes will look like. If a number of scenes are covered in single master shots, you already have the "cut-together" scenes. In some ways you are limiting your options once you get in the editing room, because you won't have all that coverage to fall back on, but if the scenes were carefully planned, you won't need it. Further, you've saved yourself from shooting a lot of unnecessary footage and the time and money that goes with it.

What often happens if a director doesn't know how he is going to cut a scene together is that he may overcover it (film as many different angles as possible). Which is akin to ordering everything on a restaurant menu and then deciding what you want to eat after it is delivered to the table. It is both expensive and messy, but it may work well for someone who has no idea what he wants and isn't particularly concerned with money.

The single master is a commitment to the final design of a scene as it is being shot. It is rooted in confidence and clarity of focus on the part of the director. Which is not to say that standard coverage isn't the way to go for certain scenes and certain films, but it's worth considering that it's not the only way to go.

Since covering a scene in a single master shot is generally faster, cheaper, and requires minimal matching, less film, and less time, you could make the argument for the brilliance of the single master shot strictly from a financial standpoint. But then when you look at the beauty, the elegance, the creative freedom offered by such a sophisticated shot, the business argument would fall to the side and it would be evident that the absolute brilliance of the single master shot lies in the creative freedom offered by the shot, in its ability to serve the art, as well as the budget and the schedule.

A scene can be covered in a single master shot using a static, or a moving camera, or a combination of the two. It can be done in a variety of ways, handheld as Woody and Carlo Di Palma did in the opening scene in *Husbands and Wives,* where the camera moved throughout the apartment, or it can be completely stationary as the actors move in front of it, as in the shot in *A Midsummer Night's Sex Comedy* where Leopold (José Ferrer) meets his colleagues on a university walkway. This particular scene called for five actors, and almost three pages of dialogue, at an exterior location in a period movie. By normal filmmaking standards, this amount of work would have required roughly a dozen camera setups and a full shooting day (instead of the few hours it took us in a single setup). But again, throwing the financial considerations aside, the scene stands on the fact that it is simply a beautiful shot.

Because of Woody's preference for the continuous master shot, several are mentioned throughout this book. The early scene in Sandy Bates's apartment in *Stardust Memories* is an elegant moving master. The long handheld sequence done in Linda Ash's apartment, in *Mighty Aphrodite,* and the "Fun at the Brook" scene in *A Midsummer Night's Sex Comedy* are also moving masters. Of course, many other directors and cinematographers use long master shots to cover scenes in film, such as the previously mentioned long car sequence done in *Children of Men,* or the one of Ethan Hawke and Gwyneth Paltrow in the restaurant and on the street in SoHo in *Great Expectations,* both of which were directed by Alfonso Cuarón and shot by Emmanuel Lubezki.

But Woody uses the single master shot in a uniquely stylized way. Often when it is not expected, when it isn't a "big" shot that will stand out and define a pivotal moment in the film. He frequently uses a single master to film ordinary moments, such as the phone conversation in the hotel room in *Stardust Memories,* or the bedroom scene in *A Midsummer Night's Sex Comedy* with Mary Steenburgen. Scenes that would have represented to most directors the opportunity, if not the obligation, for additional coverage.

If you watch Woody Allen's films, beginning with his collaboration with Gordon Willis on *Annie Hall,* you will find that the single master shot is used as a matter of course, with greater frequency and in a more stylized way than it is by many other film directors. And by working with the great cinematographers who have an extraordinary eye for framing and lighting, even ordinary, pedestrian moments in Woody's films are often designed in an inventive way, as he creates shots that encapsulate the emotion, communicate the mood, or simply present a singularly unique photographic presence, where the shot design is the most compelling element of the entire scene.

37

ASSUME NOTHING.

WHEN a scriptwriter puts pen to pad or fingers to a keyboard, most often, little thought goes into the technical details of how anything he or she might write will actually be shot. It is not the writer's job to be concerned with the "how," or to limit the story because a scene may be difficult to plan and stage. The job of the writer is to produce the best story. Period.

Think of the overwhelming nature of the big action movies and the requirements mandated by those scripts. Think *Star Wars, E.T., Titanic, Armageddon, War of the Worlds, I Am Legend.* You basically know that if you open a script and it says "Spaceship lands," or "New York City void of life," or "The sinking of the *Titanic,*" as a filmmaker you have your work cut out for you. But there are many films with scenes that seem quite simple on the surface, even ordinary and benign, yet sometimes it is these scenes that evolve into a production Armageddon or something titanic.

On *Hide and Seek,* the script called for Emily, played by Dakota Fanning, to catch a fish. Not something that at first glance would send you running for the lifeboats. Yet the dynamics of shooting that scene left us feeling like we were 600 miles southeast of Halifax and taking on water.

Contractual rules that don't allow even a fish or a bug to

be harmed while filming a movie meant working with ASPCA representatives to make sure no harm came to the fish (a trout) or the bait (a beetle) that were used in the scene. It meant that the water had to be tested, and state and county permits had to be secured to release the trout in the lake where we were filming. It meant timing how long each fish spent out of the water (a maximum of thirty seconds was allowed) and designing a way we could show Emily hook the beetle in close up, with its legs wiggling in her hands, yet not cause any harm to the bug.

To do this, the property department fabricated miniature blood packets to Velcro to the live beetles so blood would squirt out when they were hooked. On the day we shot this scene, everything was monitored by an ASPCA rep with a stopwatch to ensure the safety of the trout and the beetle. Essentially, we had a dozen adults choreographing the elements of a scene whose key component was the health and well-being of a beetle and a fish. The safety issues of the bug and the trout impacted the budget, the schedule, and the creative elements of the scene, as well. And although the fact that catering was serving trout for lunch that day never entered the equation, the hypocrisy wasn't missed by anyone.

On *Uptown Girls,* the script called for Molly Gunn, played by Brittany Murphy, to have a pet potbelly pig. Hardly the end of the world. But it did mean contracting with a breeder to produce a couple of pigs that would be the right size and age when we wanted to shoot. It also meant building an animatronic pig as a backup. Further, the live pigs had to be trained to respond to food and a clicker to facilitate performance. We then had to find a way to make "Moo" comfortable in a porcelain bathtub. None of this was easy or inexpensive.

Just because the script said "Moo takes a bubble bath" didn't mean that we could assume that Moo would cooperate. We ended up with the crew standing around a bathtub full of bubbles and a little pig who didn't like the way his hooves slipped when we placed him in the tub. It is tough to anticipate a problem like this, and tough to navigate a solution on the day of shooting, when bathing a pig can seem as challenging as the sinking of the *Titanic*.

On *Someone Like You,* the script had a scene where Jane Goodale (Ashley Judd) fantasizes about three cows in a bridal-shop window in Manhattan. When you first read that scene in the script, as a production person, you certainly pause. Again, we were stepping into treacherous water and it would take extraordinary planning and coordination between departments to pull off. Note that all of the effort that goes into filming some of these elements—the beetle in *Hide and Seek,* the pig in *Uptown Girls,* the cows in *Someone Like You*—often results in just a few minutes of screen time.

The cows presented a series of problems, beginning with getting permits to bring them into the city and solving the logistics of walking them down a New York City street. We then had to get them through the doorway of the shop and into the store window. While it may seem obvious that cows don't climb stairs or go in elevators, these are some of the things that we had to consider. We built a ramp so the cows could bypass the steps, and custom reinforced bracing to restrain them from bolting through the plate-glass window of the bridal shop. We then checked with each department to see who was best qualified to help the cows step into their costumes. Because cows don't walk up stairs, go in elevators *or* put on their own hula skirts.

Nor should you ever assume that the cows in a bridal shop will be the only challenge on any given day. This scene, shot in the downtown Manhattan neighborhood of SoHo, called for Ashley Judd and Marisa Tomei to wear hats, gloves, and winter coats. That would have been fine, except that we were shooting in July. In July in New York City, you should assume that actors wearing coats will have a tendency to melt, presenting a challenge for wardrobe, makeup, and hair. Remember, the actors are supposed to look cold up on the screen, not sweltering in their winter wardrobe.

To complicate matters further, in addition to the summer heat and dealing with the cows, we also had to make it snow. We were shackled with not only the bovines in hula skirts and our sweltering cast but with ice and water trucks, street wet-downs, and man-made flurries, as well.

So assume nothing. It will never just be cows in SoHo. It will be hula skirts and a snowstorm in July. And don't assume that you can just catch a fish or give a pig a bath simply because that is what the script calls for. Assume that there are forces of nature or, at the very least, a slew of regulations for just about everything you may want to do. Assume that you will need little blood packs for the beetles, stopwatches for the trout, and sandbags and rubber padding for the hooves of the pig. Perhaps Woody went home after the wrap without changing out of the pants he wore in the scene, leaving you without the correct wardrobe the following day, or nobody thought to ask Brittney Murphy if she knew how to swim, or the prop department never thought Hugh Jackman would crush the coffee cup at the end of take one and they foolishly didn't have backups. Whether it's something as small as a single crushed coffee cup or as large as a Guernsey cow, it will always be something. Plan for snowstorms in July, cows bolting through plate-glass windows, and the unpredictable, slippery nature of potbellied pigs' hooves against porcelain. Assume nothing.

38

NIGHT WORK; KNOW WHEN THE SUFFERING IS WORTH IT.

IF there was a single thing that could have led me to quit the film business, it would have been the night work. Unfortunately, a couple of weeks shooting dusk to dawn are par for the course on a lot of films. On a few occasions we might shoot an interior scene at night because the location is unavailable to us during the day. We might be playing the scene for daytime, rendering the night shoot a practical mandate, not a creative one. For example, on *Uptown Girls,* the department store Henri Bendel would let us shoot only after they closed. But most night shooting occurs because the scene is either an exterior at night or an interior where the camera will see the night out through a window. If you're lucky, you can schedule split calls, which means you work from ten to ten or noon to midnight, filming some shots during the day and grabbing a few more after it gets dark.

But a night shoot most likely means *all* night and begins in the late afternoon and ends with the wrap at sunrise. Add in another hour for the crew to load out equipment, often a commute on each end and a ride home that involves the radio blasting and your head thrust out the window—not for the sheer joy of the wind in your face, but just to keep you awake. Your tequila sunrise is a cocktail of 150 proof exhaustion and leaves you with a blood-alcohol level of zero, yet still driving while impaired. Your only hope lies in brisk air, loud music, and the thump of those metal strips imbedded in the tar on the shoulder of the road.

The physical pain resulting from a night shoot is only a single facet of this less than precious stone. It is a given that a tired cast and crew are less efficient. They work slowly, are prone to more mistakes and, in the case of the cast, can actually look inappropriately tired up on-screen. This exhaustion is costly. Robert Downey, Jr., did five takes in the wrong jacket one night on *The Pick-up Artist* because everyone who should have instantly realized this mistake was just too tired at 3:00 A.M. to notice.

But shooting at night costs more, and not just because the cast and crew are tired. Shooting in the dark, without any ambient sunlight, means we must light everything and we must light more. This means putting on extra electricians, renting and hauling more equipment, and spending a lot of additional time to light each scene. Which means we move slower.

Many directors make the mistake of overusing night shooting, sacrificing quality and encumbering the project with escalating costs through the inefficient management of time and money and light. In eighteen years with Woody Allen, I never saw the sunrise, and I rarely missed *The Tonight Show.*

The solution to cutting back on the physical and financial drain of night shooting can be found in several arenas. First, judicious scheduling and the split call. In the fall and winter, when the sun sets early, a 10:00 A.M. to 10:00 P.M. day leaves roughly five hours of darkness to do night work and still leaves the cast and crew with the bulk of the night to sleep. With a split call, a twelve-hour day can be scheduled with seven hours of daylight and five hours of night work. However, there are times when a split call simply won't work. You might have too much work at a location to cover it in just a few hours, but when scheduling, the split call is well worth considering.

Second, it is important to look at the script and figure out which scenes are absolutely necessary to shoot at night and which scenes can be played differently without compromising the artistic needs of the film. For example, if you establish that it is night in a shot of a couple getting out of a cab in front of restaurant in the dark, but then shoot the interior restaurant scene without a view out of the window, you can shoot the interior night scene during the daylight hours. The audience brings the assumption of night into the restaurant with that establishing shot.

Another way to manipulate the amount of night work on a picture is through shot design and coverage. Woody's style of shooting, often using a moving master instead of standard coverage, can get a scene done much faster, especially at night, when the lighting is so time-consuming.

A final and definitive way to take control of the nights is by building your sets on a stage. Which brings me, by way of example, to *Shadows and Fog*. A film that takes place entirely at night yet was shot completely during the day. Building all of the sets allowed us to turn three months of straight nights into a daytime shoot with a flick of some big studio light switches.

So when is the suffering worth it? When everyone believes that the night shoot is exactly what serves the picture best, that anything else would be an artistic compromise, and that the suffering is not a result of poor planning and less than efficient management. I've had many a director argue to shoot an interior scene at night because he doesn't understand that we won't see anything significant out of the windows. He hasn't done enough night shooting to know that we could hang flocking paper and sheers to black out the windows, shoot the scene during the day, and that it would look just like we shot it at night, rendering it faster, cheaper, and, overall, less draining.

The Big Picture

So on those pictures when you're faced with an unavoidable string of nights and you roll in at 7:00 A.M., grateful to have made it home, as you set in motion a plan that includes holding back the world long enough to get just a few hours of sleep, make sure that it is for a good reason. As you unplug the telephone, along with the rest of your life, and try to block out the fire trucks, the neighbor's dog, air traffic, and that roofer down the street, after you try earplugs, blindfolds, and medicinal scotch, you may still find that your favorite place to sleep is the floor of a walk-in-closet as you sadly admit, to anyone who asks, that you got the idea from your cat. That he likes the closet for the same reason you do: quiet, no windows. Just try to remember that before you put yourself through this— before you find yourself with a two-hour lighting job in the middle of the night, hanging your head out the car window and sleeping with your cat, first check the script. Think about split calls and building, try to shoot as much as you can during the day, and at least make sure that the suffering is worth it.

39

EARTH, WIND, AND RAIN:
YOU CAN'T IGNORE THE
FUNDAMENTAL ELEMENTS.

WHEN I am shooting a film, I check the weather forecast constantly. I know exactly what time the sun will rise and set. If my wife asks me if it's going to rain soon, she will stop me in mid-sentence and request that I answer with a simple yes or no, not give a long-winded explanation of prefrontal troughs and barometric pressure. But I know that if the wind is gusting, hair blows and sound is difficult, if not impossible, to record. And I know that we are always fighting to shoot one more setup or get one more take before we lose the light, whether to clouds or dusk or changing season. I also know that if we are shooting outside and the weather fails us, if it rains when we need the sun, that we have to have an alternative scene planned and an interior cover set available, or the unthinkable will happen: We will lose a shooting day.

I have developed the habit of using a stopwatch to time everything. Annoying, I am told, in my personal life, but of great value at work. I know how long it takes to unload the trucks, hang lights, gel windows, and set up rain towers. In a workplace populated with artists—directors, writers, cinematographers, and designers—I am serving many masters. Not just the art but also the clock, the budget, the union regulations, the rotation of the Earth . . .

Although the script for *Evening* calls for a summer wedding, we would be shooting it in the fall. I knew that the average air temperature at night in October, when we would be shooting the scene we referred to as, "the plunge," which calls for actors to jump from a thirty-foot cliff into the surf off the Rhode Island coast, would be forty-eight degrees and the water temperature in the ocean below would be in the life-threatening range. I knew that the temperature would pose problems not just for our stunt men and women who would actually jump into the ocean, but for our leading man, Patrick Wilson, who would be wearing wedding attire and repeatedly sprayed down with a Hudson sprayer, rendering him dripping wet for the better part of twelve hours. Yet I didn't know when I made the strip board and scheduled the movie that the wind would be gusting that October night at thirty miles per hour or that later that week, lacking a cover set, we would, on the fly, successfully move a scene to the leeward side of the house where we were filming while we waited for the tide to change and the wind to shift.

When I first read the script for *Evening*, I took note that the wedding reception, as written, was to be shot in a tent on the lawn of the house where we would be shooting most of the film. The house commanded a prominent point on a bluff overlooking the Atlantic Ocean. It was perched high on a cliff in Newport, Rhode Island, with the sea crashing on the rocks on three sides. When we first scouted the location, the wind was howling at forty miles per hour, which told me that it would make virtually every take we did unusable for sound. I knew that Claire Danes's hair would be everywhere except where we wanted it to be and would never match in any two shots. While I knew that we could record our dialogue when the wind cooperated and budget more time for hair, I was convinced that erecting a wedding tent large enough to hold two hundred actors out on the lawn wasn't possible. Not only would the wind tear it to shreds, but with all of our equipment the potential for injury from flying objects was high.

I was compelled to suggest that we eliminate the tent scene and shoot the sequence in a controllable interior space. Though this was a logical and obvious suggestion from a production standpoint, everyone loved the tent on a visual and creative level. From the writer, Michael Cunningham (*The Hours*), and director, Lajos Koltai, to the producers and production designer, it was exactly what everyone envisioned for the scene. But there were bigger hurdles than just the artistic one. If we moved the scene from a tent on the grounds of the estate to a reception hall, Michael Cunningham would have to change the very structure of the screenplay. In the original version of the script, a number of the guests leave the reception at the end of the night to go to the plunge—the thirty-foot cliff where the brave and/or the very drunk would leap into the churning Atlantic. But by moving the reception away from the house, the script would have to be rewritten to conclude the reception, have the actors drive in cars back to the house, then subsequently decide to go the plunge, which was a pivotal scene in the movie. The domino effect of something as simple as moving the wedding reception to an interior location presented a gale-force wind of its own.

Consider the words, "Outside the window, it is raining." A writer may like the dark or romantic feel suggested by a rainy afternoon. The director, and ultimately the viewer, will appreciate the atmosphere the rain creates on-screen, the look of wet streets coupled with the sound of rain hitting the pavement. But a filmmaker has to consider the costs and complications those words command.

Film viewers, if they ever think about it at all, will probably assume that if it is raining in a scene, then it was actually raining when the scene was shot. But this is rarely the case.

The Big Picture

Since a film is not shot in continuity, but, rather, in blocks of scenes that are logical to shoot together, scenes that are shot weeks or even months apart may end up next to one another when the film is cut together. As a result, like fitting the pieces together in a jigsaw puzzle, everything has to match seamlessly. Not only the clothing and makeup but also the weather. For example, if it is raining when an actor gets into a cab, it needs to be raining again when the actor gets out of the cab, even if the latter action is shot several months later. As a result, we generally shoot exteriors in good weather, go to interior sets in bad weather, and create the rain or snow ourselves when we want it for artistic reasons.

I know that to cover an intersection with rain—say ten thousand square feet—we will need eight special effects men, a tanker truck with five thousand gallons of water, a 150-foot construction crane with outriggers for stabilization, several hundred feet of fire hose, and one spider rig, which is a contraption made of aluminum tubing with lots of holes drilled in it. These tubes are configured like an X, with each arm about twenty-five feet in length. The spider rig is attached to the arm of the crane and then raised one hundred feet above the ground. The fire hose is attached to the rig, run down the crane arm, and is connected to a manifold that is hooked up to the tanker truck. On the day of shooting, when we are ready for it to rain, the valves are opened, the water flows through the hose to the spider rig and subsequently falls as rain. The cost for the equipment, vehicles, teamsters, and special effects people runs about fifteen thousand dollars a day.

Beside that actual expense, there are other factors to consider, as well. For example, if the rain "starts" during a scene, it means that when we "cut" the actors will have to have a change of costume and their makeup and hair dried and redone for each subsequent take. When we did a rain shot in *Someone Like*

You with Ashley Judd and Hugh Jackman, it took fifty minutes between takes to change wardrobe and redo their makeup and hair. At ten grand an hour, this is a significant expense.

Another consideration is that since rain sequences often run for a number of scenes—that is, for an entire evening or a full day in a script—it often means rain effects at numerous locations. Since we shoot out of continuity, we may need it on days four, thirty-four, forty-one, and forty-two. This, of course, presents a problem, because there is no guarantee what the weather will be like on, say, the forty-second day of shooting. What if it's a bright sunny day? If there's no cover set planned, and we have to shoot as scheduled, our rain will look pretty hokey with the sun shining in the background. And if it's New York City in December and the temperature falls below freezing, we probably won't be able to shoot the rain at all, due to safety issues. If the water freezes on the street, it would pose a risk to pedestrians and motor vehicles alike.

Clearly, those seemingly innocent words, "exterior cliff over the ocean," or "interior/exterior wedding reception," or even "outside the window, it is raining"—loom large. From the perspective of a filmmaker, the fundamental elements of Earth, wind, and rain can never be ignored.

40

FIRE AND BRIMSTONE: FULL-BODY BURNS AND THE IMPOSSIBLE SHOT.

WITH the increasing use of computers to create special effects for films, viewers may too often assume that most of what we do is accomplished in some lab. While it is becoming more common to use CGI techniques, many effects in film, to this day, are still done on the sets and on the streets, and involve difficult and dangerous elements. And there are few things in filmmaking more frightening and dangerous to do than a full-body burn.

The film *F/X* was about a special effects man in the film business named Rollie, who was played by Bryan Brown. The script called for a scene with a full-body burn. Specifically, a waiter in a restaurant carrying a flambé dessert is caught in gunfire and falls, dumping the flaming dish on a patron. The diner, in turn, was to catch on fire, leap to his feet, and struggle out of frame while burning from head to toe. Because we couldn't fake it and we couldn't realistically create it with computer graphics, we actually had to film it. We had to light somebody on fire. For this scene, we really did the full-body burn on a set with stuntmen and real fire. And certainly not without an enormous amount of planning and filmmaking illusion.

For starters, since it was mandatory to maintain complete control over the execution of the scene, we built the restaurant set on a stage, incorporating fire-retardant materials and movable walls to facilitate equipment and camera moves. Frank Ferrara, the stunt coordinator, an expert on "burns," played the role himself. (Though the stunt coordinator designs the stunt sequence, he sometimes also acts in the scene.) The waiter who handled the flaming dish and all the other actors at the table were trained stuntmen, as well.

The scene was laid out and rehearsed, approved by the director, and critiqued from every angle. The choreography was perfected down to every nuance, and careful consideration was given to planning a response in case something unexpected happened.

Another significant element in the equation was the special effects coordinator, Connie Brink. Different from the stunt coordinator, it is the effects coordinator who works behind the scenes, creating the breakable furniture (sometimes real pieces that are scored, or fabricated pieces that are made from balsa wood so that they will shatter when landed on), bullet hits, explosions, and virtually anything else a scene requires that is unusual or dangerous or must be destroyed. He works in conjunction with the propmen, preparing weapons, applying the electronically triggered squib hits, shattering windows, et cetera. Because of the amount of labor and planning involved, it must be determined in advance exactly how many bullet hits will take place in a scene, where they will be placed, and in what order they will fire. Are blood spatters, smoke, or splintering wood required? Every single detail has to be specified.

In our case, it was decided that the waiter would be shot twice in the back, so squibs were attached to his costume and the volume of the blood packets (condoms filled with fake blood) was decided. In order to be able to fire the squibs, wires were fed up the trouser legs and under the stuntman's shirt.

The Big Picture

Subsequently, when filming, these would be fired on cue in coordination with the blanks being fired from the Thompson submachine gun used by the hit man.

Preparation for the scene called for makeup, hair, and wardrobe personnel to create duplicate costumes and fire-retardant suits and hairpieces. The clothes had to look real, so that the actor could sit in the restaurant without any visible lumps from pads, wires, or protective clothing. Once "Action" was called, Frank would have to "sell it" so that the audience would totally buy what was unfolding before their eyes.

On the day of shooting, a skintight flame-retardant suit was put on the stuntman first and then covered by the actual costume, which would be treated with a flammable liquid. Any exposed skin and hair was coated with a nonflammable, water-soluble protective fluid (such as "Zel Jel") to prevent burning. Every square inch of the stuntman's body that would be vulnerable to flames was meticulously covered. Now his body could be ignited and allowed to burn for up to thirty seconds with relative safety. The only part of him left unprotected were his eyeballs, which meant that his eyes would have to be closed once he was ignited and that he would be burning, and moving, blind.

Connie and his safety team were standing by off-camera with asbestos blankets and fire extinguishers. The room was cleared of all unnecessary personnel. We rolled camera, called "action" and the door burst open. In came the hit man, machine-gun fire crackled, deafening to the ears. Stunt players dived for cover, a huge fish tank exploded, sending gallons of water cascading across the floor. The waiter was shot, he fell, Frank burst into flames. More bullet hits, people screaming. Frank was a human torch. He fell to the floor, out of frame. I called "Cut!" and Connie and his men were on him in a millisecond, putting out the fire with asbestos blankets. After the fire was extinguished and it was determined that no one was injured, a dressing crew came in to clean up the water and debris, move in new walls and furniture, and set up for additional coverage (reaction shots and inserts of bullet hits).

Of course, the most daunting of all shots are those, like the full-body burn, that pose significant, even life-threatening safety issues. The stunts that we can't completely fake and must actually stage. But every once in awhile, there are scenes that, although not dangerous, seem, at least when you first read them in the script, to be impossible to execute. For example, when the screenplay calls for something seemingly implausible, even to veteran filmmakers, like "New York City completely empty." (Think midtown Manhattan with no cars, no people, no signs of life.) And not created with plate shots and green screen and assembled in the lab using computer graphics like in *Vanilla Sky* and *I Am Legend,* but shot live in Manhattan on a day when you literally *own* the streets. For me it redefined the concept of "locking it up."

The film *The Devil's Advocate,* directed by Taylor Hackford, had a scene that required a wide shot of Fifty-seventh Street in Manhattan completely void of activity. The street vacant, as if the devil himself had erased all signs of life. Kevin Lomax, played by Keanu Reeves, had to step out of a building in midtown Manhattan and appear to be the only person in existence. Taylor wanted to "see the world," which meant a wide crane shot over the city, but with no cars, no people, no movement whatsoever. The scriptwriters undoubtedly wrote the words, "57th Street empty. No cars. No people. Just the buildings and the silence. And then a wider angle. It goes on and on. . . ." without any thought to what it would take to shoot it.

The script calls for Kevin to step out of a building and walk to the centerline of East Fifty-seventh Street, looking west. The camera was to rise up on an Aquila crane above the city so it could see ten blocks west to the Hudson River. *Aquila* is the Latin word for eagle, and indeed Taylor wanted an eagle's-eye view of Keanu on one of the busiest streets in one of the largest and most populated cities in the world, yet without another soul or vehicle in sight.

In order to execute this, there were initially meetings with the Mayor's Office of Film, the police department, and New York City traffic control. It had to be arranged with the city to shut down traffic on every avenue north and south of our location. Dozens of police and traffic officers and cars were assigned to us on the day of shooting so we could hold the city at bay. On top of that, to stop any civilians who might be on the sidewalks and streets, we had production assistants spread out over several city blocks to "lock up" and hold back the pedestrians when the time came to roll camera. This meant that in the three blocks closest to the camera, we had people in the lobbies of residential buildings, in coffee shops, and in any other buildings that might be open on the early Sunday morning when we were shooting. On the streets we left only the emergency lanes open for fire trucks and ambulances. We took a 4:30 A.M. call, had the crane built and remote head (for camera) mounted, and rehearsed the mechanics of the shot with a stand-in for Keanu while he was in makeup and hair. We put a second fixed camera on a balcony about fifteen stories high to grab another angle.

When I finally called "Lock it up" over the walkie-talkie, in less than a minute we had a clear and empty set that ran for blocks. We ended up doing four or five takes, and if you look at the scene in the film, consider that we actually shot this the old-fashioned way. By shutting down the world.

Ultimately, what makes this shot in *The Devil's Advocate* so interesting is that feat. We shot it live, on location, with an army of personnel and weeks of planning. No computer-generated images, no models or miniatures, just a lot of coordination and street work. For a few moments, we actually shut down midtown Manhattan and caught it on film. Four or five takes, two cameras rolling, and the impossible was possible: New York City rendered void of life. Likewise, in *F/X*, we really lit a man on fire. For twenty or thirty seconds, he was actually burning from head to toe. In filmmaking, despite all of our special effects and all of our visual tricks, sometimes there is simply no other way to do it than to do it for real.

41

THE SET HAS A CHEMISTRY. BIG
EGOS . . . BIG MONEY . . . BIG ART.

IMAGINE Mick Jagger in the same room with Alan Greenspan. The quintessential artist meets the head accountant. Think picric acid and sodium hydroxide or, at best, oil and water. Then toss seventy-three more people into the mix. Begin with an Oscar–winning makeup artist, a couple of teamsters, two fashion models, and a bean counter from the studio. Then add in a powerful movie director and his two assistants. Cap that off with a Hollywood megawatt star, his entourage of ten, six other well-known actors, half a dozen electricians, a helicopter pilot, a choreographer, a voice coach, and a cinematographer who speaks only Mandarin Chinese, and you can begin to get a feel for what it might be like to walk onto any given film set.

As you make your way closer to the camera, as you navigate through the artists, the technicians, through the pragmatic and the temperamental, you realize that there may not be a workplace with a more diverse population than a film set. You note that standing in the corner are a couple of friends of the director, two studio executives, the stand-in body double for the nude scene, and a cardiac surgeon who was brought in as a technical adviser. Then you notice that somebody brought their dog.

You don't recognize the rest of the people, so you start calling all of them "Moe."

Even if it's the first day of shooting, you pretty much know who is good at their job, who likes to break chops, and where the deadweight is. If it is the second day of shooting, you already have a handle on which actor won't come out of his trailer, who's going to storm off the set, who has a drug problem, who is sleeping with whom, who doesn't know their lines, and what just about everybody had for lunch yesterday.

So you broom the dog, hoping it doesn't belong to the leading man or one of the director's friends, head to the craft service table, get a decaf, and start thinking about the chemistry set you got in the seventh grade. The one that came with very specific instruction on what not to mix with what. That's when you start thinking about explosions and the chemistry of the set.

Coffee in hand, you head over to the director, announce to the crew through the walkie-talkie, "We're in in five," and exhale, not knowing whether the first little chemical reaction of the day will be a big boom or something quite benign.

While you're thinking about whose agent is going to call with a sticky complaint, you glance over your shoulder and notice a guy with long greasy hair and filthy clothes standing to the side, talking to himself. You quickly do the math, review the cast you met briefly in preproduction, and try to decide if this is a new guy in the sound department, who happens to have a Ph.D. in electrical engineering from MIT, or one of the actors in the film who's just trying to get in character. Then you briefly entertain the possibility that all is how it looks and he is, in fact, a homeless guy, or a star stalker who needs a security escort off the set.

That's when it hits you. You've been looking at your glass as half-empty, not half-full. That dirty guy leaning against the wall may have a degree from MIT or one from the streets, but if he's standing on a movie set, he probably has a pretty impressive résumé. The actress playing the part of the hooker with the impeccable Brooklyn accent may have, despite her current appearance, won three Oscars, cut her teeth doing Shakespeare in the British theater, and also be fluent in Portuguese. All the guys you're calling Moe? They're the fourth and fifth men in each department. You won't interact with them enough to learn all of their names, yet they represent an extraordinary talent pool. Among them, they have shot thousands of movies all over the world. They may have done sound for *Amadeus,* wardrobe for *Shakespeare in Love,* or stunt work for *Crouching Tiger, Hidden Dragon.*

That Hollywood megastar, the Chinese cinematographer, that producer with the deep pockets, the makeup artist working with the prosthetics, the guy sitting in the back of the prop truck? They can blow things up, make Ugly Betty beautiful, and, if the script calls for it, they can make Heidi Klum look like crap. They can, collectively, give a performance so convincing that you will believe that Cate Blanchett really is Bob Dylan, at least for the time she is on-screen. Or that Anthony Hopkins actually is a homicidal, predatory cannibal, and that Tom Hanks is a ten-year-old in a thirty-year-old's body. Or that Jack Nicholson is a colonel in the U.S. Marines, Glenn Close boiled up a pet rabbit, Michael Douglas tried to kill his wife, and Harrison Ford is the best damned president the United States has ever had. The collective talents of the people you see milling about on that set can convince you that Idi Amin is alive and well up there on screen and that James Bond jumped out of an airplane without a parachute.

Working on a film set, on any given day you are presented with a virtual periodic table of explosive possibilities. The big egos. The big money. The big potential problems that seem to follow power and fame go hand and hand with the kind of expectations that are a prerequisite if you have a contract guaranteeing a million dollars just in perks. It often leads to competition, demands, friction, posturing, stress. But don't forget that lurking behind every single big ego is a towering shadow of self-doubt. When an actor steps out of his trailer and onto the set, he may be in a ridiculous costume, or no costume at all. If his performance is not good, it may play before the world audience anyway. Actors have a lot at stake when they step in front of the camera. What if the leading lady doesn't like the leading man and you're scheduled to shoot a love scene? Or what if friction develops between your internationally acclaimed cinematographer and the award-winning director?

Standing on the set, you can almost feel it begin to simmer. Then you realize that nestled amid all these egos, all the power, and all this chemistry, somewhere among all the artists and the technicians, is a film.

So you get ready for it. The explosion of another kind all together. Not picric acid and sodium hydroxide. Not egos and attitude. But an explosion of the technical skill, hard work, and world-class talent that you were tripping over as you navigated the short distance between craft service and the camera.

Sure, the set has a chemistry, and it can be explosive, so slap on some goggles and a pair of heat-resistant gloves, turn the Bunsen burner up, check your own ego at the door, and put on a diplomatic hat. The set has a chemistry. Big egos. Big money. Big problems. But that's what comes with the territory of Big Art.

MAGIC HOUR, MAGIC MOMENTS.

42

A good deal of what we do as filmmakers involves the manipulation of light. Throughout the shooting day, the electricians haul cable and hang lights while the grips set flags and diffusion. We hide from the sun, race with the sun, wait for it to slip out from behind a cloud, or perhaps duck back behind one. All of this effort, the massive coordinated attempt to control both the natural and the artificial sources of light, is to gain some degree of supremacy over the elusive, fluid light that we so covet in film. As filmmakers, we spend endless hours trying to create and to capture very exacting light. And then every day at dusk, the sun goes and does it for us—creates twenty or thirty minutes of near-perfect light.

Magic hour. Completely unpredictable, fleeting, and brief. I've waited for it with camera crews beneath the Brooklyn Bridge, and in the canyons of Wall Street. From the Jersey shore to the streets of the Bronx. From the beaches in Rhode Island and Florida to the streets of Weehawken, New Jersey, and the boulevards of Paris, France. On the deck of a shrimp boat in South Carolina and on the street corners of Hell's kitchen.

To a filmmaker, magic hour holds the promise of magic light. Neither blazing sun nor inky darkness, just magic hour, that demarcation line between day and night. For half an hour, we get to suspend our battle and embrace a cease-fire with the sun as we surrender the camera to the warm, soft offering, that golden natural beauty defined by dusk. A single shot, say at 6:20 P.M., another take at 6:30, then 6:40, maybe one more at 6:50, and it's over as the sky fades to black.

Most everything we do in film is calculated and hard fought. We employ a herculean effort to craft just a few seconds of film, to capture that great shot, that great performance, that perfect moment. And sometimes, despite all of our coordinated, calculated and planned attempts, something broaching perfect and quite spontaneous occurs completely on its own. And not just with light. For filmmakers, there are not just magic hours but there are magic moments, as well. Some of them end up on film; others are just a still shot in the scrapbook of one's personal life. All of them fluid, unpredictable, spontaneous, brief. Just like twenty or thirty minutes of near-perfect light.

For me, it might be the experience of shooting scenes for *Mighty Aphrodite* in Taormina, Sicily, standing sandwiched between mountain and sea, between present day and the past, between Mount Etna belching smoke and the Mediterranean's turquoise spray. The set, an amphitheater built before the time of Christ, a convincing argument for the Romans' fervent belief in both the power of the gods and their reverence for the theater.

Then I might recall Jack Lemmon on *Glengarry Glen Ross* playing ragtime piano in between takes. Or watching Sir Alec Guinness play Sigmund Freud in *Lovesick* and the kids on their bikes watching us film on the streets of Queens who asked with great excitement, "Who is in the movie?"

"Sir Alec Guinness," I said. "*The Bridge on the River Kwai, Lawrence of Arabia.*" I was met with blank stares. As they rode off, leaving me possibly more disappointed than they were, it dawned on me.

The Big Picture

"Wait, Obi-Wan Kenobi!" I yelled after them. They stopped, their faces lit up, and as they enthusiastically pedaled back to watch us shoot, I knew that Sir Alec had won over another generation.

Or Robert De Niro in *Great Expectations,* the control of his emotion, as expressed in the tiny muscles of his face, truly defining a giant performance. Or the absolute privilege of spending a half hour in a motor home talking to John Huston about the making of *The African Queen.* Followed by the memory of Dakota Fanning, at age seven, delivering flawless lines take after take.

Or perhaps the afternoon spent on the bow of Tom Saccio's fishing boat on *The Prince of Tides* with Barbra Streisand, cinematographer Stephen Goldblatt, camera operator Ray De La Motte, and a cooler full of beer as we navigated the Intracoastal Waterway at sunset with nothing more to do than wait for magic hour and steal some beauty shots. A giant sea turtle covered in barnacles, dolphins forcing bait fish up onshore, an egret in the reeds. No lights, no cables, no cast. Just the rare, elusive nature of a near-perfect moment.

Then there was postproduction on *Arthur,* as a twenty-piece orchestra played "cues," the individual measures for the sound track, as scenes from the film were projected on a screen in the background while Burt Bacharach recorded "Arthur's Theme"—live.

Or the down time between takes waiting to light a scene at the Brooklyn Zoo when an animal handler appeared with a wheelbarrow full of pumpkins and started throwing them like softballs into the mittlike mouth of a hippopotamus, one after another, serving neither a curveball nor a fastball, but certainly putting a new spin on lunch. A flash to a bobcat crossing the road on a scout in New Mexico. A sailfish that shot out of the water and into the air on *Great Expectations.*

Or simply bearing witness to those great comedic mountains, ranging from Dudley Moore in *Arthur,* to Tom Hanks in *Big,* Art Carney in *Going in Style.* Woody Allen every day. An ongoing private audience with all of them, a collection of moments that never made it into a film, defining instead a lifetime spent standing in the foothills of a laugh.

Then there is Al Pacino "in character." Vanessa Redgrave saying just about anything. Or Woody, who is so synonymous with the Upper East Side that he looks out of place standing anywhere outside of Manhattan, visibly lost without the East River by his side and a New York sidewalk beneath his feet.

Or five A.M. after a night shoot, driving by that place in Queens near the Midtown Tunnel where you can see the sun coming up on the Manhattan skyline and smell the bread baking at a local bakery if you happen to hit it just right.

The memory of flying to the Vineyard with Sydney Pollack at the controls of his Learjet. Or to East Hampton on a Citation from Gainesville, Florida, for lunch with Arne Glimcher on *Just Cause.*

Or Kate Nelligan transforming from a young woman to a sixty-five year old as much from the change in her voice, the way she carried her frame and how she held her hands, as from the five hours spent in the makeup chair. Scouting artists' lofts near Montmartre in Paris. Or working with Keye Luke, "Number One Son" from the Charlie Chan movies, a half-century later, when he was eighty-five. And seeing Sir John Wood doing Tom Stoppard plays in London during the seventies, then working with him more than a decade later on *The Purple Rose of Cairo* and *Sabrina.* Or shooting *The Nutcracker* and the chance to work with the New York City Ballet—no actors, no dialogue, no reverses, just five cameras and a few months of dance. A regular date with the Polichinelles, Darcy Kistler, Peter Martins, and Tchaikovsky.

The Big Picture

Then there was the chance to share filmmaking with an audience of teenage boys as we shot in a prison in Memphis, Tennessee. Every one of them in for murder, serving twenty-five years to life, and still able to smile. Or perhaps a single look of hope on any of the faces of the indigent and disabled when shooting at Goldwater Hospital on Roosevelt Island or at Lenox Hill, Montefiore, or Mount Sinai.

Filmmaking, in truth, is elaborate cinematic illusion. But unlike the magician on the stage or the actor in a play, filmmakers get much more time and many more chances to shape the finished product. And as the camera is rolling and we chase the light, and perhaps make it rain, we are hoping to craft just a few seconds of perfection and capture it on film. Every single element in the frame has to be perfect. Not only the physical action in the scene and the delivery of the lines but also the background movement of the extras, the wardrobe, the set dressing, and the recording of sound. Ultimately, the director gets to assemble, to buff and polish the finished product in the editing room . . . shot selection, computer and sound effects, music. But the component parts, the physical pieces of film that the director takes with him into that editing room, are assembled, piecemeal, over many months while we shoot principal photography. And while what we do is usually so planned and precise, so crafted and extracted, there are, every once in awhile, those magic hours and magic moments. Like when we were shooting *Evening* in Newport, Rhode Island, and a storm appeared over the Atlantic, nature like a great theatrical actor stepping onto our stage, claiming a moment all its own. That storm brought the biting wind and driving rain that we tracked relentlessly those days as we awaited our scheduled night shoots, but also delivered a cinematographer's dream: a colorful and dramatic sky. But that is filmmaking. Both the hardwired and the soft-focused. The meticulously planned and painstakingly executed, accompanied by both unpredictable complications and fortuitous opportunity.

As filmmakers collect the footage for those films we will all see in the theaters, we are also collecting our own personal outtakes. Culled from the thousands and thousands of hours, and all of the takes that never got printed, from all of the scenes that never got shot, there are thousands and thousands of moments that will always be remembered. A lifetime of near-perfect light, some magic hours and magic moments, not just for the screen but to claim as our own.

43

. . . BUT IT'S NOT ALL
AUTOGRAPHS AND SUNGLASSES.

WORKING in film production might leave you standing just a few steps from the bright lights of Hollywood, but it also puts you close enough to know that most of that perceived glamour is as staged and fabricated as the performances, that period wardrobe, and those elaborate stunts. The red carpet, the movie premiers, the photographs of limousines and yachts—those forty-karat moments you see on television and in magazines—are often just another production number, a planned and necessary marketing tool to hype product. The film industry may sport a golden halo, but the reality of the shoot is often more a crown of thorns than a priceless tiara, more Blood, Sweat and Tears than Harry Winston.

Put twenty or thirty worn-out cast and crew members on a hundred-degree set, shut all the windows and doors, add a few buckets of putrid animal blood distributed over the walls and furniture, and let loose 25,000 blackflies and any pretence of glamour instantly fades. Then, while everyone is holding their noses and swatting flies off their sweaty arms and faces, ask them to dress the set, adjust lights, operate a camera, or deliver a performance. This is about as far from glamorous as you can get, and while it might not be listed in the dictionary under *misery,* it defines the word for me. When your skin stops crawling from the decidedly unpleasant reality

180

of this scene (which we shot as Sean Connery discovered two corpses in *Just Cause*), consider spending a day inside a walk-in refrigerator in an inner-city morgue. Even though you've done it before, are surrounded by a forest of lighting and grip equipment, and are working with a couple of high-powered movie stars, no matter how hard you try to think otherwise, you're still in a morgue. While those corpses lined up on gurneys on the day of shooting may be plastic mannequins or extras from the Screen Actors Guild, the recently deceased were lying right there when you scouted the location a few weeks ago, and no amount of disinfectant can wipe that fact from your head. The next twelve hours find you desperately trying not to touch anything, disgusted by the thought of lunch, and reluctant to even breathe.

It seems that we work in either hot, crowded rooms or out in the elements. If the wind isn't blowing an icy rain off the ocean in February, then the Florida sun is so hot the windows are cracking in that fishing shack we've managed to cram half the cast and crew into for the day. These debilitating working conditions, these physically dangerous or emotionally tough locations, weigh most heavily on the crew, who can't escape to the comfort of motor homes. But the cast doesn't get off scot-free, either. If it was twelve degrees out on that balcony when the electricians were hanging the lights, it's likely to be twelve degrees when the actress in the evening gown is out there performing the scene as well. Yet "uncomfortable and unpleasant" are only the front end of this equation. There are also serious safety concerns when we shoot in these circumstances.

Safety lanes sound like something reserved for the highway, but we have them on film sets, too. Mandated by the sheer size of the cast and crew, the cramped quarters, the mountains of equipment, the flammable building materials and wardrobe, and that generator pumping high-voltage electricity onto the jerry-rigged, stopgap, gaffer-taped world of that film set. Toss into the mix the added complication of stunts that may involve fire or falls, car chases and aerial work, explosions or gunfire, and you have a recipe for disaster. During the decade between 1990 and 2000, over forty people died on movie sets. Crane collapses, motorcycle mishaps, helicopter crashes, gun accidents. . . .

Unless you are filming the whole movie in a studio, shooting a film is never just another day at the office. Virtually every scene and every location present something unknown that should send you running for both the OSHA (Occupational Safety and Health Administration) and the Red Cross handbooks. The stakes are high when you put a film crew on a rooftop fifty stories above the street, as we did on *The Devil's Advocate,* or at a functioning smelting plant, as we did on *Manhattan Murder Mystery.*

Shooting in the subway comes with mandatory attendance at "train school," an eight-hour crash course in "New York underground" where the realities of working with live subway cars, the third rail, and on a train bed covered with iron dust and heavy-metal filings are not lost on anyone. Nor is the quick lesson in arcing electrical current and its attraction to metal-toed shoes and any equipment not wrapped in rubber.

Shooting in the Everglades necessitates a brief seminar on amphibious reptiles, predatory invertebrates, and meteorology. A truncated course covering wildlife-avoidance techniques, followed by the fundamentals of alligators, fire ants, brown recluse spiders, water moccasins, scorpions, heatstroke, and lightning strikes. It leaves you calculating how long it will take to clear the set if there is an electrical storm or where to land a medevac helicopter should the need arise. Setting background in the Catskill Mountains when the air temperature is five degrees below zero better find you able to protect yourself against frostbite. And hopefully you are on your toes when shooting in a prison, where you must review procedures in case of an incident or "lockdown" and follow the rules about no cell phones, no eye contact, no sharp objects, no shorts or revealing clothing.

And that smelting plant in New Jersey where they crush cars and melt them into molten steel? Pretty much, you're on your own. There is no two-hour course offered on the ABC's of blast furnaces and toxic fumes or on commonsense procedure when around two-thousand-degree heat.

Sometimes it is easy to see how to take something that is dangerous and make it safe. When one director wanted to hang a twelve-year-old actor from the fifth-floor ledge of a factory building, we had him stand on an apple box and "hang" from the first-floor ledge instead. With all risk of injury eliminated, any fear on his face was just good acting. But often it isn't that simple.

Some scenes and some stunts, even though they are planned and choreographed with all the movie resources and tricks of the trade we can muster, are still inherently dangerous. Jumping a car over an open drawbridge at seventy miles per hour is never safe. Most running shots look best at between twenty and twenty-five miles per hour, but some directors want to run the car faster. Which means the crew members traveling on the back of the open insert car are put in greater jeopardy. Safety is compromised with each uptick in speed, each added foot of elevation.

On the rooftop of a fifty-story building, you and your equipment have to be tethered if the wind is above fifteen miles per hour. Yet the truth is, at that height you may find yourself wanting to be tethered even if the air is completely still. Then there are the bad neighborhoods, the gang-controlled blocks, airport runways, the horse track, the deadly, whirring blades of a helicopter. And that's just the controlled danger. There are also the surprises. The taxicab that careens onto the set, the collapsed scaffolding, the plate-glass bank windows that shattered from the heat of the lights on *Quick Change*. The misfired explosion on *Soup for One,* or when a "gag" went wrong on *F/X* and the hood of a car was unintentionally blown three stories into the air.

For every day you get to shoot at Tavern on the Green or in a restaurant in Rome or the Trocadero, there will be a week at a garbage dump or gasoline refinery or on the open water. And on that film set, with a collective mind-set permeated by an almost religious belief that we can and must do anything to get the shot, it is sometimes hard to remember that we can't defy all the laws of nature. That just like the hood of the car on *F/X,* the simple premise "What goes up must come down" still applies, and most of that perceived glamour of the shoot is just as fabricated as the rest of the movie. As Gordon Willis liked to say about filmmaking, "It's not all autographs and sunglasses. But it sure beats mining coal for a living."

44

"POOR MAN'S PROCESS":
CONSIDER WAYS TO GO "CHEAP."

MOST movies have scenes that involve filming in moving vehicles. There are basically three ways to get these shots. Perhaps the most common way is what is called running shots, which involves mounting a camera on a "picture car" and either towing or driving it out on the streets with the actors inside. This has the advantage of providing the live background outside of the windows, but the disadvantage of limited camera angles and the obvious issues of the uncontrollable nature of the elements, from potholes and traffic to weather. We sometimes do running shots on the live streets, as we did in *Glengarry Glen Ross* when we towed Jack Lemmon around Queens, and we sometimes shut segments of the roads down, as we did in *Nothing But the Truth* when we drove a school bus full of children on a major thoroughfare in Memphis, Tennessee.

Shutting the roads down takes a lot of planning and coordination, but it provides a safer environment for everyone involved, allows for consistent speed, and is mandatory if you are doing any unusual maneuvers. Running shots can look very realistic, but they are time-consuming and therefore expensive. If the camera is mounted on the side of the car, or frontally through the windshield and operated remotely, it provides only static shots. If the car is on a process trailer (a low flatbed) the camera can be manually operated and provide more intricate shots, but each setup still takes from two to three hours. The culprit is really workable space. The actors have to be lit in a confined area, the car is typically engulfed in equipment, and work is done one department at a time, instead of simultaneously, because a soundman can't be setting a microphone in the car at the same time as an electrician or grip or assistant cameraman is doing his job.

Process photography is another traditional way of filming sequences involving moving vehicles. It entails shooting "process plates," which are shots of the roadway or background for the scene, from several angles and then projecting these plates on a screen on a stage while the actors sit in a stationary car. A fan blows the hair, the driver steers and brakes according to the contours of the road, and the scripted action and sound effects of traffic are added in postproduction. Many older films that used this technique come to mind, including *To Catch a Thief,* in which Cary Grant and Grace Kelly race along the serpentine roads of the French Riviera in a sports car. While not visually perfect, it works, and during the 1950s, when this film was made, it was relatively high-tech. Modern process-plate photography looks, of course, much better than it used to. In *Stardust Memories,* Woody and Gordon Willis opted to shoot plates along the Jersey shore, and to do rear-screen projection for several scenes. We shot our scenes on a stage in Manhattan, with the actors seated in a Rolls-Royce and the background projected behind them. Simply put, if a shot was to last for thirty seconds, we would need a plate of at least that length to play in the background. Also, for every angle Woody wanted to shoot, a corresponding plate had to have been shot, developed, and printed and on hand to be projected (that is, front, rear, or profile). By shooting in this manner, DP Gordon Willis had the ability to light in a controlled environment. No sun or clouds to battle, no wind or rain to contend with.

Of equal importance is the fact that this method of filming afforded the flexibility to do more diverse camera angles
than towing would have allowed. For instance, for one setup
the camera was mounted on a small slide on the hood of the
Rolls, allowing it to dolly back and forth, from chauffeur to
passenger, in a single fluid motion. The restriction of a tied-
off, or static, camera was eliminated, along with potholes,
road bumps, sun glare, and engine sounds over the dialogue.

The more modern and technologically advanced method
of achieving the same effect is to shoot the actors in a studio
against a green screen. Then later, in postproduction, background plates are added, seamlessly completing the sequence.
It is less cumbersome and time-consuming than rear-screen
projection, and the technology allows for a very realistic look.
This means that you can film your actors in a car in Memphis
and marry them to the streets of Washington, D.C., in postproduction, as we did for *Nothing But the Truth.*

Since these shots all involve working in the confines of a
car, and usually shooting close-ups, the camera reads very little outside the window, and what is there is usually out of
focus. If you are willing to forgo the daytime exterior view
outside the car window and shoot your car sequences at night,
there is a third, much more economical, way to get moving vehicle shots. Something aptly called "poor man's process." It is
just what it sounds like: a method of doing process shots simply and inexpensively. It works only for night scenes and involves putting the picture car on a stage or in a warehouse,
blacking out, and then simulating traffic lights, headlights, and
other background elements. On *Radio Days,* Woody and Carlo
Di Palma used "poor man's" for a scene in which Aunt Bea
(Dianne Wiest) ends up in a car that runs out of gas on Breezy
Point. The car was rocked and swayed by the props to simu-
late movement, and fog was added, providing the illusion that

the actors were driving at night out by the ocean. And once the car "stopped" the camera was able to pull back and reveal it on the edge of the reeds by a sand dune. (All shot on stage during the day.) By shooting "poor man's" there was no need for a plate crew to shoot process plates, there was no time-consuming towing and rigging, nor were the actors having their close-ups filmed at four o'clock in the morning, when they would have been punchy and exhausted. Rather, we shot during the day, were able to control the fog and wind and lighting, and had the option of doing diverse camera angles.

If you can't afford green screen, computer graphics, or plate units, think poor man's. Similarly, if you can't afford a crane, have your operator shoot from the top of a ladder or the roof of a truck. No money in your small budget for a dolly and track? Try putting the operator in a wheelchair or an open car. Steadicam too expensive? Go handheld with a wide-angle lens (so you won't have to pull focus and any jarring movement will be diminished).

There are lots of alternative ways to film shots for movies, and deciding how best to cover a scene always represents a challenge. It is ultimately a balance between the practical and the creative, between what you want and what you can afford. Between knowing where to spend the money and where to "go cheap."

45

SWEAT THE SMALL STUFF ...
ROUTINELY.

EVERY film project rises like a cinematic house of cards. The foundation is laid in preproduction: the script, the crew, the cast, the set design, the schedule, the director's leadership and vision. If there are cracks or inherent flaws in this foundation, the project may be headed for creative or financial doom from the very beginning. But even if we get the big, early stuff right, the ultimate success of the project is equally dependent on the dozens of small logistical and creative choices that are made over the course of every single day. Success or failure often hidden within the slew of small decisions made in the deceptive calm of preproduction or rendered during the rapid-fire, frenetic days when we are shooting.

While a film, unlike a literal house of cards, can't be felled with a single metaphorical brush of a hand, each day is a revolving door, a carousel of potentially small setbacks nestled between creative opportunities: an unacceptable change in the weather, the loss of a location, a malfunctioning piece of equipment, an actor uncomfortable with his lines. Or that break in the cloud cover when we were shooting *Evening,* which gave us a chance to grab an unexpected sunset. Or the sudden surprise rainsquall that worked so effectively when shooting *Great Expectations* in Florida as the character Lustig, played by Robert De Niro, was being hauled into jail. All of these, mere stumbling blocks or unbridled opportunity, with each solution found in the bankroll of technical knowledge and ingenuity, professional expertise, managerial skills, and the pure artistic talent that define and embody the cast and crew.

Some of these small decisions are hard fought, some reluctant compromise, some straight business, others pure art. With the correct solution all of these decisions result in, at worst, nothing more than some lost time and a series of dings and dents to the budget and, at best, they result in a great shot and a seized opportunity. So we reschedule, reload, rewind, reshoot, reexamine, resolve. But collectively, a string of poor, seemingly small decisions can deliver a catastrophic blow to a project, rendering it a financial or creative failure, and our house of cards collapses.

On *Going in Style,* Art Carney stumbled, hit his head, and got a black eye. He was needed in virtually every scene, so we couldn't shoot around him, and the bruise was too dark, the eye too swollen, to cover with makeup. In this case, we had no choice but to shut the production down for a couple of weeks and wait until it healed. Even with insurance, this cost the company hundreds of thousands of dollars given the deductible, the rented studio space, pay or play deals with actors, equipment costs, salaries for department heads, the cost of hotels, et cetera. It also put the bulk of the crew out of work during the hiatus. This started with a simple stumble and a black eye, and while the consequences were huge from a financial standpoint, our choices were limited.

But more often than not, the solutions are not so definitive, so undeniably self-evident. We must weigh the odds, calculate the risk. Will the sun pop back out in a few minutes, or should we move to a cover set because those clouds overhead are here to stay? Do we spend money to create snow for continuity, just in case it snows when we are shooting two months from now, or take the gamble that it won't snow at all, or that we can remove it from the location if it does? If the freight elevator is stuck and the superintendent is not in the building, do we break for lunch and buy ourselves an hour? Or can we resort to the stairs? Or wait and hope he returns in a few minutes? If the director wants to grab a beauty shot before the day's work can he be convinced to get the big dialogue scene first because it makes more financial sense? Or will we end the day with the crew in double time and behind schedule and with not much more to show for our work than a superfluous shot of the bent grass covered in morning dew?

Will someone think to get the camera crew to use a new magazine for the second take when shooting that intricate stunt sequence, just in case the first one is ruined in the lab? If the director decides to have the camera pan to the right, which will mean we have to move all of our equipment trucks, will someone notice that if we pan to the left we can cover the scene just as well and buy ourselves back an hour? And that extra hour? Will it save us a meal penalty, and some expensive overtime, or allow us to grab that shot the director was hoping to add on, if we had the time at the end of the shooting day?

What do you do if the camera truck is stuck in the sand or the crane arm is broken? Perhaps Ashley Judd is lost somewhere in the subway. Barbra Streisand has a pimple, Harrison Ford decides to wash his hair. On the surface, each of these events is solvable, some more readily than others. Whether you get it right or you get it wrong, more often than not the ripple effect will be felt throughout the day and in some cases throughout the film. Indeed, in many cases it will be seen up on the screen as well.

Many of these small decisions affect the financial bottom line. Did we make the day's work? Will the film come in on budget? But the director will be faced with a litany of daily decisions that have an impact beyond the dollars and cents. Some begin as problems, others as opportunities. Are the walls the right color? Does he absolutely have to have a crane? A Steadicam? An extra shooting day? How are the performances? The choreography? The lighting? The look of the extras? The delivery of that last line?

A good director has to know where and when he can compromise, what he can give up and when to stand his ground. On *Stardust Memories,* Woody wanted an extra with a large nose and strong profile for the alien spaceship landing scene at the end of the film. He couldn't find someone with the look he wanted among the hundred extras sent over by casting, so he made the creative decision to reschedule and shoot the scene on a different day. Glenn Close arrived on the set of *Evening* with a broken leg. Lajos Koltai, the director, who cast her knowing this, had to decide how to design shots to work around her injury. How would he cover the critical dance scene with Buddy (Hugh Dancy)? We ended up shooting her sitting down with the cast off, or standing with the frame line above the knee when the cast was on. Watching the film, you may notice that she doesn't move around all that much, even when dancing.

A director will face thousands of seemingly small creative decisions that will, to some degree or other, make their way up onto the screen even if it's in the form of that shot you couldn't get because of time lost on something else.

Every project will eventually find its place somewhere along a continuum ranging from the brilliantly successful to the catastrophically flawed. Each film judged by the box office draw and the sharp pencils of both critics and studio accountants. Failure can be predetermined when the foundation is laid with either a poor script or the wrong cast, a weak director or production team. But even if you get these things right, failure can creep up on you with the day-to-day mishandling of a thousand small things. When approached with both painstaking precision and at least a small amount of trepidation, each decision and ultimately each scene becomes a carefully placed card supported by those beneath, dependant on those yet to come. As we embrace each problem and each opportunity and build our house of cards, we defy economic, artistic, sometimes even physical gravity, relying on the structural support offered by the combined talents of the crew, and, more often than not, by the adhesive nature of buckets of money.

So sweat the small stuff. Routinely. Both the logistical and the creative. Defy gravity and build a cinematic house of cards that will stand up to the friction and the downward pressure that define the process of filmmaking.

46

FILMMAKING IS ALWAYS ABOUT
BOTH THE ART AND THE MONEY.

WHETHER framed as an intellectual argument or a practical concern, the two driving forces behind film, art and money, are contradictory by nature, or at best a counter-intuitive combination. Although it would be easy to argue that in many commercial films there is not enough focus on the art, there is no disputing the fact that film-production costs are, across the board, staggering, or that, within the industry, commercial success often trumps artistic merit.

In fact, it is an undeniable reality that filmmaking as an art form is sadly caught in the duel wake of stratospheric production costs and blockbuster expectations. Unbelievably, even a ten- to twenty-million-dollar project is considered "low budget," a fact that can leave the independent filmmaker who is funded with a paltry few million feeling like he is bringing pennies to a high-stakes poker game, and where creativity is constantly swimming in that backwash of budget and schedule and finds itself giving way to the hard reality of high flying expenses. The dynamics of the budget inevitably leaving the director to navigate those narrow straits where artistic vision meets commercial venture, where the freshwater purity of art is catastrophically tainted by the constant inflow of business brine.

As a result, a filmmaker who sets out to make that feature

film with less than optimum financing, trying to circumnavigate the cinematic globe on "Team Low Budget," better have an oceangoing constitution and be fitted with enough determination to provide the stabilizing force of a lead ballast keel. The independent filmmaker had better be battened down and braced for the blunt force of the financial wind that can tip the art of film on its creative rails, because that small, independent, "low budget" film will find itself sailing right next to the big budget films from "Team Studio." All of which may leave a small independent filmmaker feeling like he entered the America's Cup race with a dingy named *Compromise*.

The opening scene of your script may read "Int./Ext. Church Wedding" and you may conjure up a grandiose vision of St. Patrick's Cathedral in midtown Manhattan. After all, you're thinking GRAND sequence. Perhaps starting with an aerial shot following a motorcade of antique Rolls-Royces through the city streets, then a crane shot from high above the church, followed by a Steadicam floating in through the front doors and up to the bride and groom at the altar. You're thinking beautiful light filtered down through stained-glass windows, and the rarefied opulence of a cathedral. You're thinking elaborate set design, lavish flowers, a handmade wedding dress, hundreds of extras.

What your budget dictates however, is a small church on a side street in Queens, fifty extras, meager set dressing, no antique cars, no crane, no helicopter. And not a roomy two days to shoot the scene, but an impossibly tight six hours.

It's page one, scene one, and already a giant compromise. All of a sudden, you're sailing in a financial windstorm and on day one your creative sails have been ripped to shreds. You are the director, and for you, it is all about the art. As you begin to try to salvage the film creatively, you realize that while you may make it through these rough seas intact, when you are finished what you have artistically may not be the film you originally envisioned.

But there is another side to this story. If you happen to be hired to sail a ship for Team Studio, to helm one of the sleek, multihulled, financially stable pictures that come with a huge budget, you may be compromising in a different but equally challenging way. You may find yourself, just like the character of the playwright David Shayne, (John Cusack) in Woody Allen's *Bullets Over Broadway.* Shayne loses artistic control of his project when "the money" demands that he cast the floozy girlfriend, Olive (Jennifer Tilly), of mob boss Nick Valenti (Joe Viterelli), who put up the money to produce the play. The fact that Olive is completely wrong for the part, has no talent, can't pronounce the dialogue, let alone memorize it, or be believable in the role of a psychiatrist is seemingly irrelevant.

Unless you are a really "big-gun" director, one of the rare few who has the power to maintain creative control, the studio will have substantial creative input all along the way, as well as final cut on the film. That film you were offered to helm may come with actors you wouldn't have cast already attached to it. Not because some mob boss wants his talentless girlfriend to be a star, but perhaps because the less than perfect actor the studio wants for the part has a name that will mean something in foreign presales. You may find yourself losing the film creatively, not because of the budget, but because of the studio's team approach. Or because of the politics involved in trying to sustain a career in a business where you are only as good as the numbers behind your last picture's opening weekend. A business where new writers are routinely brought in to rework dialogue or add scenes, where the studio watches dailies, approves casting decisions, and conducts focus groups to make sure that the audience likes what you did with the project. And if they don't, if those focus groups aren't pleased with your work and have a few ideas of their own, you might be sent back to change the ending or reshoot some scenes to make the film "better."

All of a sudden, you realize that you are making a commercial film and it's not your project. You're not an artist answering to no one but yourself; you are simply an employee. And your film is not going to debut in the gilded world of the art-house gallery, but in the big-box supermarket that is the American multiplex.

And so begins the almost daily struggle between art and budget that defines filmmaking. The different dynamics between owning your project and sharing ownership with a studio, or between getting what you want and getting what you can afford. Between collaboration and compromise.

Now, multiply this dynamic by the literally hundreds of compromises you will make while directing a film. From casting and locations to shooting days and final cut. From music and number of camera setups to wardrobe and release dates. Some of these compromises will be yours alone; others will be forced upon you by the laws of physics, the constraints of the budget, or the studio. If you attempt to maintain creative control of a project by building it from scratch, by writing the script and raising the financing yourself, you will, more often than not, find yourself creatively restricted by the limitations of the budget. Yet if you are offered a chance to direct a studio project, you will have to live with the choices that come from above and hope for more creative control next time. Or, as Helen Sinclair (Dianne Wiest) so wistfully and dramatically states to David Shayne in a toast as he laments about losing creative control of his play in *Bullets Over Broadway,* "To an ideal world with no compromise." Until then, there is no denying that filmmaking is always about both the art and the money.

47

OR IS IT? THE AUTEUR FILMMAKER VERSUS THE GUN FOR HIRE.

THERE is a third type of filmmaker. Not the studio "gun for hire" handed a script and a project that comes creatively hemmed in, often after spending years in development, and not the true indie filmmaker with the severely restricted budget. But the auteur filmmaker, an elite distinction written about by Andrew Sarris, a film critic for the *Village Voice,* in his essay "Notes on the Auteur Theory in 1962." Sarris classifies certain filmmakers as auteurs by recognizing those artists with a body of work that is not only technically well crafted but is characterized by a signature underlying message and a definitive personal style. European filmmaking is defined by them: Jean Renoir, Bernardo Bertolucci, Federico Fellini, Jean-Luc Godard, François Truffaut . . . And despite the dominance of big Hollywood studio films, the United States has produced an admirable crop of its own auteurs, including Charlie Chaplin, Orson Welles, Martin Scorsese, and Woody Allen.

But in an industry so fueled by commercialism, why do we care about personal style, about message, and a body of work? After all, the American studio system, which produces giant, commercial, blockbuster films, has also opened the doors for some directors who do both art and commercial films extremely well. Directors who walk the line between art film and commercial venture with extraordinary brilliance and virtually unlimited funding. Some of these directors make big commercial films and they make big studio "art" films as well. They are rendered so powerful by their commercial successes that they answer to no one when it comes to their art. Steven Spielberg can make a commercial film like *E.T.: The Extra-Terrestrial,* as well as *Amistad* and *Schindler's List.* Martin Scorsese can make commercial films like *The Departed* and *Goodfellas,* as well as *The Age of Innocence.*

But as good as these films are, as technically perfect and high-concept, as indisputably well funded and artistically crafted, no matter how important their message, they are still made for a commercial audience. Which leaves room for filmmakers who do not have the box-office draw of a Hollywood giant but who can also maintain complete creative control over their work and be free of concerns over commercial success. Granted, these auteur filmmakers will always have the financial restraints of a budget, but no studio will be in the wings watching dailies, suggesting bringing on a writer, approving casting decisions, or reshooting the ending. And while we will always go to the multiplex to see films by Martin Scorsese and Steven Spielberg, some film viewers want to go to the single-plex, the art house, and see the filmmaker's version of haute couture, the art film. A no-holds-barred, pull out all the stops, break the rules, push the creative envelope, and stretch the fabric of design, film.

Why do we care about Woody Allen, who has received criticism for not showing up to collect Oscars, not making commercial films, not making funny films, not drawing at the box office—basically, for not trying to please anyone but himself? Why do we care about such self-indulgent disregard for the consumerism of film?

Because we believe that what he does is important, in terms of both message and style, regardless of its commercial or critical success. And because we believe what he does is important, we don't want him to stop. That we need filmmakers who are not answering to the people in Kansas, or Hollywood, the people on Wall Street, or to those with an office on a back lot. The auteur filmmaker. The filmmaker without shackles to a financier's bottom line, or pulled in by the reins of studio executives or who is vulnerable to critical opinion, popular opinion or box-office draw. A filmmaker who can make films like *Interiors* and *Stardust Memories,* like *Husbands and Wives* and *Crimes and Misdemeanors,* and not be afraid that they may fail. We are even willing to be indulgent viewers and wade through what we might personally perceive to be their failures for their great defining films.

Every filmmaker is judged by two standards: the quality of the art, and the box office draw. Except for the very few who have earned the right to stand by art alone. Those exceptional auteur filmmakers like Woody Allen who don't have to show anybody, anywhere, their script. Who have total freedom for casting, editing, final cut—any cut. Who are not employee but employer. Who have the freedom to reshoot and recast, to ignore the Oscars, the box office, the critics and all of the business brine. Those artists who have proven they can enter the America's Cup Race in a handcrafted vessel of their own design and come in first.

We want filmmakers who will make "haute couture" films, that unwearable and even sometimes unwatchable material, marching it down the cinematic runway without ever looking back, without ever caring about what anybody thinks, because film is, after all, art. We want someone out there with a camera making films, not just engaging in a business venture. Films like *Z,* by Costa-Gavras, and *Fateless,* by Lajos Koltai, come to mind. We want the contradictory and the counterintuitive—artists working in film. As Rob Reiner's character, Sheldon Flender, proposes in *Bullets Over Broadway* (a film Woody wanted to call *The Artist* but couldn't because the title was unavailable), "Let's say there was a burning building and you could rush in and you could save only one thing. Either the last known copy of Shakespeare's plays or some anonymous human being. What would you do?" He proposes that at least some of us would go for the art. And when the hit man, Cheech, takes Olive down to the dock and shoots her to keep her from ruining the play, we may laugh at the absurdity, while we inwardly applaud his allegiance to the purity and importance of his art.

IF YOU'RE NOT IN A UNION, YOU PROBABLY WON'T GET TO WORK ON A FEATURE FILM.

THE truth? If you write a script, sell it to a production company, and attach yourself as the director, then plan on joining the Writers Guild and the Directors Guild of America. Want to be a television or film actor? You have to join the Screen Actors Guild or you can't get hired. Want to do makeup or hair on a feature film? If you're making a film in New York, you have to be in Local 798. Still photographer or camera assistant? Local 600. Want to drive a truck? The Teamsters Local is 817. And if you want to operate a generator, dress a set, or carry a hammer on a feature film set, go see them down at the stagehands' union, Local 52. While there are a few exceptions to this rule, like working as a production assistant, or on a low-budget, nonsignatory film, or in a "right to work" state like North Carolina or Tennessee, where films sometimes pick up nonunion drivers, grips, and electricians, virtually everyone working on the set of a feature film is in a union.

Making a film involves tons and tons of heavy equipment. It sometimes involves dangerous stunts, such as car chases, explosions, and full-body burns. As filmmakers, we routinely work with fire, weapons, children, and 220-volt electricity. In addition to being potentially dangerous, what we do is extremely technical and expensive. So we have to be exact and precise. Mistakes are just too costly on every level. We need to be staffed with experienced professionals, and it is the unions who provide these highly trained individuals.

The contracts with each of the ten or more unions that may be represented on a motion picture set are often several hundred pages long. Are some of the rules encumbering and tough to navigate? Exclusionary? Sure they are. But walking time, kit rental, the third man, golden time—all exist to protect the union members.

Need to hang a light on set? You'll need a union electrician. However, if you have to move a couch to hang that light, it will have to be moved by a set dresser, because the electrician isn't supposed to touch it. If the DP wants to set a flag or "cutter" in front of that light, the contract mandates that you have a grip to do that. Then, if you plan on placing a coffee cup on the table next to that couch, you have to call in a propman, because, by union contract, nobody else can handle that cup on set. Sound ridiculous? It really isn't. There are reasons for all these rules. No one can touch that coffee cup except a propman, because we need to know it is exactly where it should be for continuity. If the electrician moves it, and neglects to put it back exactly as it was before, with the exact amount of liquid and the same lipstick mark, facing exactly the same way, our subsequent shots will not match.

To do my job as an assistant director, you have to spend two years in a training program or accumulate over five hundred days as a production assistant before you can apply to join the Directors Guild. Then there are years of "firsts." First green screen, first diva, first explosion, first helicopter shot, first elephant on the beach . . .

Since a key factor of my job is navigating the morass of union rules, when I interview people to work on my production staff, I often ask this question: "If you're shooting with forty extras for seventeen hours in Far Rockaway on the Friday before a holiday and wrap them at two A.M., knowing that they will work the following Tuesday, what must you do?"

A. Provide them with the same meals the crew gets.
B. Pay them travel time.
C. Bus them to Grand Central Station at the wrap.
D. Pay them an additional day's pay for the holiday.
E. Give them an additional day's pay for each hour worked over sixteen.
F. All of the above.

If they answer, "All of the above," they have a good chance of getting hired.

Interested in becoming a camera operator? A typical route would be to train for a year at a camera house just to learn about the equipment. Then you would work as a loader for another year or more to learn your way around a film set. This will qualify you to work as a second assistant cameraman and, eventually, a first A.C. Finally, after all that training and experience, and several more years, you may start making the transition to operator, providing there are some DPs around willing to give you a chance. These are hardly jobs you can just step into.

In a business prone to sporadic employment, impossible hours, and grueling working conditions, all of these rules are designed to protect the union members. Some protect their livelihood, while others, like turnaround and meal penalties, actually protect their lives.

The bottom line? Decide what you want to do and learn a craft. Specialize, whether it is in acting, editing, sound mixing, production, camera or set design. Join a union so that one day, when you are working on that feature film and the production company wants to push through and shoot until sunrise, they will be paying you a union-negotiated wage and guaranteeing that you get a ten-hour turnaround so you don't get killed by falling asleep at the wheel on your way home. Not only will that union train you; they will fund your retirement, provide health and disability insurance, keep track of residual payments, and, in some cases, even send your kids to college. But if you're not in a union, you won't get to work on a feature film.

49

HIRE THE BEST CREW.
THE TEAMSTERS MATTER.

THINK the transportation coordinator or Teamster captain or drivers aren't important to a film? A single ride to the airport with one of them will probably change your mind. A few simple stories will convince you that the transportation department on a film does a lot more than drive the cast and crew vans.

The transportation coordinator, like every other department head, reads the script in preproduction, reviews the shooting schedule, and prepares a budget for the department. He considers the size of the cast and crew, the number of locations, and the distances between them. How many crew vans does he need? How many rental cars? How many drivers? What about motor homes for the actors or "honey wagons" (portable dressing rooms and bathrooms)? How many stake-bed trucks to transport equipment and how many picture cars will be needed for the film?

On any given day that we are shooting, the transportation coordinator or Teamster captain is responsible for making sure that every single person, whether cast or crew—roughly about one hundred people—will arrive exactly where they need to, on time and without a glitch.

If the transportation coordinator isn't good at his job and there aren't enough vans to get the crew back from lunch exactly on time, or the actors are late for the call because there are miscalculations on the traffic, or pieces of equipment aren't delivered to locations on time, how many hours and how much money do you think you could lose over a fifty-day shoot? If it was just a single hour a day among the thirty or forty drivers, all the pickups, all the dropoffs of equipment, that would be over a half a million dollars in lost shooting time. For a single lost hour each day of our fifty-day shoot.

Transportation is often the largest line item in a film's budget, running over a million dollars on some feature films. Having the best people behind the scenes and behind the wheel can save the company a lot of money. This is true for each and every department—construction, wardrobe, property. The "time is money" equation that I have been pounding home is extremely significant here. The meter is running at ten to fifteen thousand dollars an hour when we shoot. At this hourly rate, you want the very best working for you in every single department.

But I promised you stories from that ride to the airport. Not number crunching. On one particular trip, the teamster captain was pissed off because the line producer had just asked him either to move into cheaper housing or to pay, out of pocket, the thirteen dollars a day that his out-of-town housing was over what they had budgeted for him.

Any sane person has to think, She actually asked him to give her thirteen dollars a day? Over the course of a fifty-day shoot, that would be $650. Six hundred fifty dollars to not piss off the guy who is making equipment package deals, signing the time cards, approving the overtime for thirty or forty drivers, and is responsible for delivering the cast and crew to the set throughout the day.

To save $650, that line producer had just made an enemy out of the guy responsible for managing and spending that huge number listed next to "Transportation" on the top sheet of the budget. Six hundred fifty dollars represents less than four minutes in a shooting day.

"Do you know how quickly I could make that money back if I wanted to?" he said to me.

And of course I did. I've seen many department heads who are ticked off or annoyed by something "throw out the anchor." We quickly start feeling the drag. This guy wouldn't have to do anything more than linger at a red light to cost this line producer $650. But she was too shortsighted and, quite frankly, too inexperienced to figure that out.

Two filmmakers in a car for an hour, we talked shop. Initially, we commiserated about this film, since both of us hated it, but the talk quickly turned to other projects. His and mine, but mostly his—both of us trying hard not to think about the thirteen dollars.

He told me about shooting *Miami Vice* in the slums of the Dominican Republic. The location so dangerous that the director traveled with a security detail armed with machine guns. In a particularly harrowing event, a crazed and angry local showed up on one of the sets with a gun and opened fire. In a tense and uncertain moment, the gunman was shot and killed by one of the film's security guards. "There was a lot of lead flying around on that job," the teamster captain said. But I was thinking that thirteen is a prime number and only divisible by one and itself.

I told him that when we were shooting *Just Cause* in Miami, Florida, we needed a solid half mile of vertical parking to accommodate the trucks we used for a single scene of two people talking in a kitchen. He shook his head in appreciation of the sheer lunacy of what I had just said. A half mile of vertical parking, for two people in a kitchen talking. Almost more unbelievable, more absurd, than gunfire on the set of *Miami Vice* or asking a department head for thirteen dollars.

He told me about the time he was shooting a film in

Oregon, in the mountains at an elevation of nine thousand feet. They had placed a picture car on a mountain pass, left it sitting on top of sections of chain-link fence so the wheels would still have traction, something to grab hold of if it snowed. And it did. Thirty-nine inches' worth the night before that scene was to be shot. His boss handed him some snowshoes and sent him, before the call, to warm up that car sitting on the chain-link fence in that mountain pass, so the actors wouldn't be cold while filming the scene. Up to his shoulders in drifting snow, wearing snowshoes for the first time in his life, huffing and puffing in the thin oxygen at nine-thousand-foot elevation, he headed out to warm up the car for the actors. As he was telling me this, I was thinking that thirteen is a factor of thirty-nine. That thirty-nine is thirteen times three.

Then he told me that the helicopter pilot that brought in equipment and took the film off of the mountain for the lab couldn't take off—not enough air—until he removed some weight from the chopper. "Not enough air," he repeated. He still couldn't believe it. High altitude, like bad management, could be a little suffocating, I thought. Neither one of us could stop thinking about the thirteen dollars and how much it was going to cost that line producer back at the office, having a latte and not realizing that thirteen was such an unlucky number.

It's hard to imagine when you are sitting in the theater what might have gone into any individual shot in a film. Whether it is half a mile of vertical parking needed for the trucks, or a hike in snowshoes through the mountains, or flying bullets in the streets of a Third World country, the film viewer will never know, can't possibly know, about the huffing and puffing, the drifts of snow, the grounded choppers, the flying lead, or the thirteen dollars.

But the producers? The director? They know. And they

should want to make sure that every member of the crew is, first and foremost, the absolute best at their job. Then they should make sure that, to a man, each member of that crew feels respected, both professionally and personally. Genuinely, not superficially. Demonstratively, publicly, and without question. Anything transparent will have about as much traction as sheet ice.

This respect should be rooted in the fact that, without a doubt, in one form or another, the production company will be asking each member of the crew to strap on some snowshoes and walk through shoulder-high drifts for them. And it will often be to do something as thankless as warming up a car, or hauling cable to a distant site, or any one of the thousands of other invisible tasks that are the backbone of film production.

At nine thousand feet, with a grounded chopper and snowdrifts, a crew huffing and puffing in the high elevation and low oxygen that defines a movie shoot, you do not want the crew thinking about the thirteen dollars the company just screwed them over for. When they face the mountainous movie passes, and flying lead, when they make equipment deals, or fill out time cards, when they sit at red lights, you want them to be thinking about hoisting the main sail and flying a jib, not throwing out an anchor. Above all, you want them to know that you believe their contribution matters.

Because it does.

When I worked with Woody Allen, he always had the best crew in New York. World class, in every department. He both gave and got respect. It registered both on the bottom line and up on the screen.

And while he hired the best crew, shot in flat light, forgot about the monitor, sweated the small stuff, shot on a low floor, kept the script to one hundred pages, warped time, stole some shots, faced the realities of the budget, and knew the value of an unrehearsed scene, the very best part about shooting with Woody?

Lunch.

50

ALWAYS HAVE A NICE LUNCH.

I know what you're thinking: Come on, have a nice lunch? When we're shooting, the production company will spend upward of three thousand dollars a week just on snacks. You read that right. *Snacks.* Three thousand dollars a week for M&M's, hot dogs, Oreos, chips—and that's just to tide us over. When we show up on location at 6:00 A.M., the caterer is preparing breakfast. Burritos, coffee, omelettes to order, rolls and pastry—whatever we want. And the buffet continues all day. With so much food constantly available, how can lunch really be that important?

Think back to first grade. A cupcake in your lunch box made your day. Let's face it: Nothing ever really changes. Lunch is pretty important to everybody. Even to an eighty-man crew shooting a movie and surrounded by snacks, lunch looms large. And not just for the food but also for the "recess." It may not be a game of tag on the playground, but it's thirty to sixty minutes off your feet. The grips, the set dressers, the camera assistants—they all do backbreaking physical labor, often in difficult conditions: extreme heat, freezing cold, close quarters. They need food and they need to rest. So much so that rules about lunch are spelled out in the union contracts. Every detail, down to the minute.

If the production company isn't providing a catered

meal, the crew must be given lunch money and break for one hour, plus walking time—five to ten minutes on each end of the meal to get to and from a restaurant. If there is a caterer, the crew can break for thirty minutes for lunch, but the clock doesn't start running until the last person gets through the catering line. This is serious stuff. So much so, that we time it on a stopwatch. At ten to fifteen thousand dollars per hour to shoot, every minute adds up.

Break for lunch six hours after the call? Great. Break six hours and one minute after the call and you just bought a meal penalty, which means that every minute for every person on the crew just got more expensive. Often, somebody back in the office then calls the studio, and the cost efficiency of that decision to buy a meal penalty will have to be justified. This may be lunch, but it's not kids' stuff. It's contractually regulated and taken seriously by both workingman and studio alike.

The math gets tricky. Let's say the director wants to do one more shot before you break. You're the AD running the set. You know that if you don't break the crew now, that one more shot is going to cost the company an extra few thousand dollars. If the director needs the shot, and you can't grab it after lunch or next week because you will no longer be at the location or one of the actors will be wrapped and unavailable, it makes sense to buy the two-thousand-dollar meal penalty and get the shot regardless of the cost. Doing it this way may, in fact, cost less than it would to come back at a later time, load in, light, block, and shoot it with a crew in straight time. There's your justification for that meal penalty. On the other hand, you may know that the shot the director wants would be easy to get at the end of the following day, or even at a different location, and that it is way too expensive to buy the penalty and get the shot now.

The Big Picture

But all of this talk of union rules and punching the clock just gets us to the front door of lunch. If I were to free-associate, provide some random musings about lunch over the last thirty years, I wouldn't be thinking about meal penalties and catered food. Nor would I be thinking about union contracts, walking time, or lunch money. Just like your average first grader, I'd be thinking a slightly upgraded version of cupcakes and recess. Which in my case might begin with eating pizza in a motor home with Art Carney. Hot, greasy, funny. No. Hilarious. Think private audience with Norton from *The Honeymooners*. Just throw in a quart of soda and a large pie. Move on to George Burns and a solid hour, a virtual run-on sentence of jokes. The man barely stopped to swallow.

Then my mind might head over to Twenty-one or The Four Seasons with Woody Allen, Tony Roberts, or Michael Caine. Calamari, grilled polenta, pan roasted red snapper. Then there's thirty straight days at Shun Lee West with Woody and Mia, Brian Hamill, Jane Martin and Carlo Di Palma (who *really* didn't like Chinese food). Then a flash of Nick Nolte and Barbra Streisand eating corn on the cob in the South Carolina heat. The Carnegie Deli, which has both the best corned beef and the biggest sandwiches I've ever seen, pops into my head. Or the opulence of the Russian Tea Room contrasted with a memory of Woody ordering Mac and cheese al dente at the Tarrytown Howard Johnson's. A flash of a little old lady with a gift of a large zucchini. Sven Nykvist and Max von Sydow reminiscing about Sweden and their lunches with Ingmar Bergman. Le Bernardin, Il Nido, Gage and Tollner. The pompano at Piccolo Venezia. Then there is the trail of people approaching the table for autographs and pictures. Ilona boiling water for pasta in Robert De Niro's motor home. Gordon Willis sitting alone, eating liverwurst. Me, defrosting myself in a hotel room in Atlantic City. A sandwich out on the rocks by the ocean in Newport, Rhode Island. A plate of food in the back of the prop truck. Nathan's on Coney Island. Sicily. Rome. New Jersey. A prison yard, a sidewalk café.

And I'd be thinking about Paris. The French crews break for an hour and half: three courses, red wine, café au lait. Or New York again: John's Pizza, Mezzogiorno, the front seat of my car. Then I'd be thinking about the lunchtime birthday pranks—the strippers, erotic cakes, the catered lamb chops and crab legs. Lunch on a stoop in Brooklyn or with Harrison Ford and Sydney Pollack in a restaurant on Martha's Vineyard, or on a park bench anywhere in the sun.

I wouldn't be thinking about looking at my watch and getting the check because we're "back in" in seven minutes. I'd be thinking about *lunch* and the playground of New York. The all-access pass and the keys to the city. Any restaurant we want, no jacket and tie required, no reservations, no waiting line. Just lunch. Great conversation, great food, great friends . . . An updated version of cupcakes and recess. Bill Murray got it right when he looked down at his plate of swordfish at the Ocean Club and said, "I guess this is about as good as it gets."

But after all the glitz and glamour, my heart will always be back with the crew. With the tired arms and weary legs, the sore backs and pulled ligaments that justify the union mandate of walking time and meal penalties. The importance of a nice lunch arises from the cold, hard reality of twelve-hour days and night work. Defined not by shrimp and white wine, but by the sheer weight of those bright lights that hang on a movie set and the men and women who load the trucks, haul cable, lay dolly track, or run with a sixty-pound Steadicam strapped to their bodies. Lunch for me will always be a stream of memories, with more of them seeded in a folding chair than a velvet seat. *Always have a nice lunch.*

GLOSSARY OF FILM TERMS

Learn the language of the set.

ABBY SINGER: The second-to-last shot of the day, named for an AD / production manager who had a reputation for announcing the last shot and then adding one more.

APPLE BOX: A wooden box approximately twenty inches by twelve inches by eight inches in size, used for cast and crew to sit, stand, or place equipment on. Additionally, there are half apples, quarter apples, and one-eighth apples in conforming dimensions.

AQUILA CRANE: A lightweight camera crane that can rise up to 120 feet in the air. *Aquila* is the Latin word for eagle.

ARRIFLEX: A camera-manufacturing company and rental house founded in Germany.

ASA RATING: American Standards Association scale of measurement for film speed (the light sensitivity of a particular stock).

BANJO: A spreader used to stabilize a camera tripod.

BARN DOORS: A fixture on lighting units consisting of four flaps that can be folded in or out to alter or cut the throw of the light.

BASHER: A small light mounted directly over a camera lens for soft, direct facial lighting.

BAZOOKA: A cylindrical pedestal used to mount a camera on.

BLONDE: A 1000- to 2000-watt open-faced light.

BOOKENDING SCENES: A vernacular term for the scenes that precede or follow any particular scene in a script.

CHINA BALL: A Chinese lantern with a soft light inside, often used to enhance the lighting for close-ups.

COOKALORIS (AKA COOKIE): A flat board with patterns cut into it, which when placed in front of a lamp creates shadow patterns.

COUNT BASSIE: Means "one more time," or another take on the same setup.

COVERAGE: A term referring to all the camera setups utilized to film a scene.

CTO (COLOR TEMPERATURE ORANGE): Colored gels used to convert daylight (5400K) to tungsten (3200K.) A correction for standard interior lighting.

DAILIES (AKA RUSHES): The previous day's printed takes, which are viewed by the director and other key crew members.

DEUCE: A 2 K, or two-kilowatt, light.

DOUBLE NET: Nets are screens inserted into the front of a lamp to lower its intensity. Sizes include singles and half singles as well as doubles. Also refers to grip nets, which are set with century stands and placed in front of lights for diffusion.

DOUGHNUT: An approximately four-inch-square piece of wood with a center hole cut out in order to hold and stabilize the wheels on certain light stands.

DRESSED: A term meaning the set is physically prepared for shooting. All furniture and inanimate objects are in place. (These elements are referred to as "set dressing.")

DROP AND PICK UP RULE: A clause in the SAG contract that outlines rules for payment for consecutive employment. An actor may work one day, be idle for ten days, then work once more, but he is paid only for the two days that he actually worked. If idle for less than ten days, he must be paid for the entire time period.

DUVETYN: Black cloth used to block ambient light from doors and windows, eliminate reflections, etc.

ELEPHANT EAR: A steel plate or running board attached to the side of a camera dolly for the AC or operator to stand on.

F.D.R.: A reference to Franklin Delano Roosevelt's New Deal. It means "We've finished this shot and are moving on to the next one."

FINGER: A small flag used to cast a shadow or cut light.

FISH POLE: A long, lightweight boom to attach a microphone to.

5 K: A five-kilowatt light. (Other lamp sizes are 1 K, 2 K, 10 K, etc.)

FLOCKING PAPER: Black paper used to black out windows and eliminate ambient light.

GATE: The opening on a camera that the film actually passes through. The gate is checked after every setup for hair or fibers that will flaw the print.

GIRAFFE: A maneuverable, lightweight camera crane.

GREEN SCREEN: Refers to the process of photographing a subject in front of a green screen so that it can be placed over a different background in postproduction.

GYRO: A mount used for camera balance and stability when doing helicopter or other unstable shots.

HMI (HALOGEN METAL INCANDESCENCE): Lamps balanced for daylight photography (5400 degrees K.)

INKY-DINK (AKA INKY): A small incandescent accent light.

ITALIAN TRACK: Lightweight dolly track, including curved sections, often used for interior shots.

JUMP CUT: An editing term defining a cut within a single shot. The elimination of these frames produces a jarring visual effect.

KENO FLO: A lighting unit utilizing banks of daylight or tungsten tubes.

LAVALIER: A wireless microphone typically hidden in the actor's wardrobe to record sound.

LOCKED OFF / TIED OFF: Means the camera is physically locked in position and will not move during the shot.

LOUMA CRANE: A camera crane with a telescoping arm and a remote head effective for arming and moving in confined areas (over a crowded room or through a window, for example).

MARTINI: Term for the last shot of the day. May also be referred to as the window or L.F.S.

MOE: A term of reference, particularly in New York, for anyone on a movie set whose name you don't know or can't remember—as in "Watch your back, Moe."

MOLE FAN: An eighteen-inch near-silent stage fan used for wind FX.

M.O.S. (MICROPHONE OFF SET): Means that no sound will be recorded. (Often erroneously said to mean "Mitt out sound," as expressed by an anonymous German director.)

PANCAKE: A piece of one-inch plywood cut to the same dimensions as an apple box. Used to elevate equipment, set dressing, actors, etc. Also called a one-eighth apple.

PAY OR PLAY DEAL: A contractual agreement between a production company and an actor or crew member that guarantees payment for a specific period of time even if the project is abandoned or production is pushed off to a later date.

PICTURE CAR: An automobile that is being photographed in a film.

PIGEON: A metal disk with a stud to secure a lighting unit to.

REDHEAD: A small 650- to 1000-watt lamp often used as a fill light.

RITTER FAN: A large, powerful fan (seventy-two-inch blades) for wind effects.

SCREEN DIRECTION: The direction anything in frame is moving, or anyone is looking—for instance, left to right or right to left.

SCRIM: A sheet of material put in front of a light to diffuse it.

SEX AND TRAVEL: Means "F—k off. Clear the lens. Get out of the way.

SHOTMAKER: A customized vehicle used for "running shots" (shots of moving vehicles), with a variety of options for camera mounts, equipment, and personnel.

SIDES: A term for the actual physical pages for a particular scene in the script.

SPIDER RIG: A device used to create rain effects in films. An X-shaped pair of aluminum tubes with holes drilled in them, they are suspended over the set and water is pumped through them.

SPLIT CALL: A crew call for midday that allows half of the day to be shot in daylight and the second half at night.

SPLIT DIOPTER: A camera lens with two focal distances, it allows two subjects in different parts of the frame to be in focus simultaneously.

TABLE READ: An informal reading of the script—around a table rather than on a set—attended by the cast and some key crew members at the end of preproduction.

TABLEAU / PROSCENIUM STYLE: A shot composition created when the camera is locked off, thus holding a static frame reminiscent of a proscenium theater.

TECHNOCRANE: A large, stable camera crane with a telescoping arm of about twenty-five feet in length, used with a remote head and ideal for arming over and above a set—for example, the ocean, a cliff, or a city street).

THREE-DAY RULE: A general rule of thumb helpful in deciding if a production company should build a set or shoot on a practical location. More than three days of shooting on one set may justify construction costs.

TITAN II CRANE: A crane mounted on a truck and having wheels that can "crab." It is mobile and can be used on rough terrain. The camera is operated conventionally—by an operator and an AC—and the arm may be maneuvered by a grip.

TRACING PAPER: Translucent paper put in front of lights for diffusion.

TROMBONE: A fixture hung over the top of a wall on a built film set to hang a light from.

TUNGSTEN: Refers to the filament of lighting units used for interior lighting. Color temperature: 3200 degrees K.

UBANGI: An offset extension plate attached to a dolly for mounting a camera.

GLOSSARY OF FILM TERMS

ULTRA-DINO: Large lighting unit for exterior work, configured with multiple (thirty-six) bulbs.

VARIAC: Like a rheostat, allows the intensity of a light to be altered incrementally.

WIGWAG: A device with reflector arms used on back lots to stop traffic. Like small railroad crossing lights, they signify "Cameras are rolling. Quiet."

WINNIE: A Winnebago motor home used for dressing rooms.

INDEX

INDEX

INDEX

INDEX

wind, shooting in the, 160
window, 220
Winkler, Irwin, 2, 15, 95
Winnie (Winnebago), 223
The Wizard of Oz, 30, 66
Wolski, Dariusz, 48
Wood, Sir John, 177
wranglers, 35

writers, not concerned with
"how," 151
Writers Guild of America, 78, 202

Y Tu Mamá También, 6

Z, 200
Zelig, 45, 46